# CREATIVE
# *Loving*

# CREATIVE
# Loving

AN INSPIRING GUIDE TO THE
ART OF MAKING LOVE

CARROLL & GRAF PUBLISHERS INC, NEW YORK

This edition first published in 1996 by
Carroll & Graf Publishers, Inc.
260 Fifth Avenue
New York, NY 10001

Produced by Marshall Cavendish Books, London

ISBN 0-7867-0320-2

Library of Congress Cataloging-in-Publication Data is available

Printed and bound in Italy

Some of this material has previously appeared in the Marshall Cavendish partwork *LOVER'S GUIDE*.

# Contents

# *Introduction*

*CREATIVE LOVING has been written to help loving couples*

*enjoy the sexual side of their relationship.*

*Making love is after all one of the most profound ways of being close*

*to another person, and a vital ingredient in many happy partnerships.*

*This book describes some of the ways you can get more enjoyment*

*out of the most intimate side of your life, and create an*

*even greater bond between you and your partner.*

Sexual relationships can become stale, and less fulfilling than they were at first - due not so much to incompatability between the partners but to problems of communication and simple lack of knowledge. For most of us there is a whole world of sexual practice still to discover. This book encourages you to discuss your physical needs with your partner, and gives you the facts you need to improve your sex life.

The subject is discussed with complete frankness and honesty. You will find here information about topics that are hard for many of us to discuss openly, even with those closest to us. You will discover how to develop sensitivity to your own body, and how to help your lover do this for you too. You will also find new ways of pleasing your partner, both emotionally and physically, so together you can enjoy an enhanced physical relationship. You could find you reap many benefits from this in other aspects of your life

*Foreplay* describes how most people need to be in the right mood to enjoy satisfying sex. It tells how with thought, care and tenderness men and women can prepare each other for love.

*Loving Positions* outlines some of the most popular positions that people enjoy when making love, and some exciting variations on them.

*Perfect Orgasms* gives information about how partners can bring each other to orgasm. Techniques for reaching simultaneous orgasm are described, although it is emphasized that this is really for skilled lovers, and should not be regarded as the primary goal of love.

*Enjoying Sex* lays emphasis on the great variety of lovemaking techniques, and tells of how different postions make it possible to enjoy different types of pleasure.

*Sex and Romance* gives some suggestions for keeping the sparkle in your relationship, and describes ways for men and women to communicate with each other when it comes to romance.

*Overcoming Problems* shows how difficulties can be resolved if couples talk openly to each other, and make sure they take the trouble to sort things out together.

# 1

# Foreplay

Most men and women want more from making love than the simple satisfying of a physical need. All of us can make sex a more intense experience by lingering over the initial stages, and by taking the time to arouse partners fully. Skillful lovers enjoy gently controlling each other's enjoyment, and find foreplay greatly increases their pleasure. There is an infinity of ways to create excitement, the choice is yours.

# IN THE MOOD

*Arousing your partner in special ways before lovemaking can pay dividends in the form of better and more intense orgasms for them – and for you.*

The value of foreplay to increase the breadth and scope of lovemaking has been recognized for thousands of years.

The Ancient Chinese recommended that the man should delay his orgasm until after the woman had experienced hers – even if it meant that it did not happen at all. This was largely for religious reasons, but the principles of anticipating your partner's needs rather than your own still hold true today.

### AFTER A WHILE

The media generally see long-term relationships as being stale and boring, whereas young lovers are seen as dramatic and passionate.

Certainly, the biggest enemy to successful sexual relations is boredom, but then again familiarity between a couple can mean real strength. By knowing an individual's unique needs, their partner can exploit them and turn foreplay into a memorable experience.

### A TIME AND A PLACE

Making love is more about what goes on in a person's head than what happens biologically. That is why illicit affairs can be so appealing. Yet so often the sex in an affair – heightened with danger and guilt – is unsatisfactory for both parties.

For the couple who have difficulty in finding time for each other, it is as well to remember those early days when they could not keep away from each other. The sex was probably unsatisfactory – but there was more emphasis on touch, loving words, gifts and surprises.

▶ *The sensitive woman can up the tempo of foreplay and bring it down, always remaining one step ahead of her partner. Not only will this increase the chances of reaching simultaneous orgasm, but the delay will increase its intensity.*

▼ *If a woman is slow to arouse sexually, then the man must compensate by delaying his own climax and increasing the pace of her arousal. To do this the method of foreplay has to be what she likes best.*

It made sex more exciting, and, without it, sex can all too easily become routine.

### DO THINGS TOGETHER

Almost anything can act as an appetizer to love if the mood is right. A shared hobby, such as sporting activities, can easily lend itself to creative foreplay. Certainly, such activities release endorphins – chemicals that make us feel good. And, after a highly charged game, sex can easily follow on.

### USING EROTICA

Although there is no substitute for your own body as a means of arousing your partner, erotica has its place. It can come in many forms – books, magazines, films, or art – and a couple do not need to spend vast amounts of money to achieve the desired effect.

*MY GIRLFRIEND LOVES TO BE SPANKED DURING FOREPLAY. I GET HER TO LIE OVER MY KNEES WHILE I GENTLY SPANK AND FONDLE BOTH HER BUTTOCKS. THIS DRIVES HER WILD AND HER PASSION REALLY GETS ME GOING.*

### VERBAL FOREPLAY

The accomplished seducer knows the value of compliments and flattery. It is not so much what is said, but the fact that someone we are attracted to has made an agreeable comment. And if we are told that we look good, we are not going to disbelieve it.

**◄ Make sure the water is running at a comfortable temperature and do not use too much pressure when washing her vulva.**

**▼ Not only is kissing an important part of foreplay, it can also be used as a gentle way to re-arouse your lover.**

### SEX GAMES

Couples may use sex games as part of foreplay from time to time. These can

▲ *Your partner's buttocks and her perineum are both highly sensitive areas – use your tongue and your lips to kiss and caress them. Better still, if she has a vibrator, gently massage the perineum with it.*

vary from board games to more specifically tantalizing games that a couple already enjoy. Whatever the game – from dressing up to stripping off – its purpose is straightforward.

## FOR HER

The most skilled foreplay can leave any woman unsatisfied if the mood is wrong.

Given that the woman's orgasm is primary and the man's secondary, what follows is a list of suggestions for getting

*NOW AND AGAIN, MY PARTNER AND I DECIDE TO ACT OUT AN IMAGINARY SCENE SUCH AS DOCTOR AND NURSE. WE BOTH LIKE DRESSING UP AND WE FIND THAT IT'S A MEMORABLE WAY TO SPICE UP OUR LOVEMAKING FROM TIME TO TIME.*

▶ *Kiss her all over her body, from the top of her head to the tips of her toes. With time, you will discover that your woman has many highly sensitive areas over her body. Many women in particular find that having their toes sucked is highly arousing.*

your woman in the mood for love. Each can be adapted to suit individual needs, but none should be rushed.

### SHOWER TOGETHER

Personal hygiene is an essential requisite for good sex, and a shower is particularly suitable for setting the mood for love. Pour your partner a small drink and start the shower for her. Slowly remove her clothes – kissing and caressing her as you do so.

Wash her hair using your fingertips to rub in the shampoo and then rinse as sensuously as you can. A lover's hands that are in no hurry can be an arousing taster of what is to come.

Now, do her back and neck while the shower sprays water over her. If your shower is in a bath, sit on the edge and take each leg in turn into your lap, soaping it thoroughly. Stand up again and lather her breasts. Apply generous quantities to her buttocks and then use a small amount – too much soap can sting – to slowly wash her vulva.

When you have finished, detach the shower spray and rinse her. Apply the nozzle very close to her skin, using the jets of warm water to tantalize her. Pay spe-

## WINE AND FOOD

WINE AND FOOD CAN BE USED TO WONDERFUL EFFECT DURING FOREPLAY. NOT ONLY CAN THEY HELP TO SET THE MOOD – A SMALL DRINK BEFORE LOVEMAKING RELAXES BOTH PARTNERS, AND GOOD FOOD CAN ACT AS A REAL APHRODISIAC TO MOST COUPLES – BUT THEY CAN ALSO BE USED AS SEX AIDS. FOR INSTANCE, THE SHAPE, SMELL, TEXTURE, AND TEMPERATURE OF THE FOOD OR LIQUID YOU ARE USING CAN CREATE A WEALTH OF EROTIC SENSATIONS THAT CAN MAKE FOREPLAY TRULY MEMORABLE.

TRY EATING FOOD DIRECTLY FROM DIFFERENT PARTS OF EACH OTHER'S BODIES. YOU CAN PLACE SOFT FRUIT, HONEY – OR WINE – ON YOUR PARTNER'S GENITALS OR BREASTS AND THEN LICK IT OFF. NOT ONLY IS IT DELIGHTFUL FOR THE RECIPIENT AND THE GIVER – IT IS ALSO A DELICIOUSLY DECADENT FEELING FOR BOTH.

cial attention to her breasts – many women find this highly erotic.

Save the rinsing of her vulva until last, but do not spray too powerfully. Then rub her down with a warm towel, ensuring that every part of her is dry.

### USE YOUR PENIS
Massage is highly erotic but a man has other foreplay methods. Lie your partner down and use your eyelashes or hair to trace a carpet of sensation over her body.

▼ *Teasing and tantalizing your partner can be a wonderfully arousing build-up to lovemaking.*

Use your penis to trace a path around her lips and then her breasts and rub it into them, paying special attention to her nipples. Use it to tease her buttocks and perineum. If you both like a little mild bondage these sensations can be exaggerated if she is restrained.

### BREAST PLAY
Many women's breasts are highly sensitive during arousal. Ice can be wonderfully shocking if it is rubbed around each nipple. The woman can dangle her breasts in her lover's face as he kisses them. Wine, yogurt or even ice cream can be placed on them while an attentive lover licks them off.

Some women like semen over their breasts. If you masturbate yourself, you can then direct the fluid onto her breasts and rub it in for her.

### BUTTOCK PLAY
A woman's buttocks are highly erogenous. The perineum is delightfully sensitive and is often totally ignored.

Lay your partner down, with a couple of cushions under her bottom. You can find out how sensitive her perineum is by licking and kissing it.

Alternatively, some women like having their but-

# CREATIVE LOVING

▶ *Try kissing your man all over, starting at his feet and toes and working up to his face, saving his genitals until last. Men are sensitive in the most surprising areas. Ask him to tell you what he likes best.*

▼ *Using your breasts to massage your partner's body will be a new and pleasurable sensation for both of you.*

tocks lightly spanked. Of course, trust is essential between both partners for this.

## FOR HIM

If the mood is right, most men can be brought to orgasm in seconds. Yet, with skillful foreplay, it can be delayed for ages.

If your man has fantasies about you dressed in a particular way, indulge him once in a while. It does not devalue you in his eyes, and in any case, most men find a semi-clothed woman sexier than a naked one.

## BATHING

Giving a man a bath can be an exciting way to bring him to the verge of orgasm. Soap his front down gently, avoiding his penis, using long strokes. Then ask him to turn over and wash the backs of his legs. With his buttocks raised, use a finger to wash his perineum. Use light strokes, and a slow, persistent, pressure. Now, turn him over and wash his penis and testicles. Pull back his foreskin, if he has one, and briefly simulate masturbation. Ignore any pleas to bring him to orgasm at this stage, then dry him with a warm towel and take him to another room to finally make love.

## BREAST PLAY

Your breasts can be used to provide exquisite sensations for your partner. Lie him back naked, lean over him and use your breasts to trace a path over his body. Move one breast around his penis. On his back, trace a path from head to toe and run an erect nipple along his perineum.

Run your breasts over

*▶ Give your partner a tongue bath – if you drink some iced water or wine before you do this, the chill of your tongue will add extra sensation. Alternatively, yogurt or even ice cream can be placed on the body and then licked off.*

his face and allow him to take your nipples into his mouth if he wants to.

Apply a little oil to your breasts and flatten them over his penis, taking it between them. With rhythmic movements, bring him to the verge of orgasm.

### USE YOUR LIPS

Use your lips to kiss him all over, paying special attention to his genitals, but without taking his penis into your mouth. Kiss his feet and toes, and let him see what you are doing. Work your way up his leg, by-pass the genitals and kiss his nipples. Then descend slowly towards his penis, breathing close to his skin as you do so. Take his testicles into your mouth one by one.

### USING YOUR VAGINA

Perhaps the most intimate form of kissing is for a woman to use her vaginal lips. If your vagina needs moist-

ening apply a small amount of oil or KY jelly. Then kiss him with your vagina, starting from his feet and working up to his face. The scent of your vagina and the unique intimacy of the act is highly exciting for both partners. Finally, linger over his face before giving him a full genital kiss on the mouth.

### SEX AIDS

There is room in the armoury of all lovers for sex aids – not as a substitute but as enhancers. A vibrator is traditionally used to bring a woman to orgasm but it can also be used on men.

Try using it on his nipples and then turning him over and teasing his buttocks with it. Above all, be imaginative. ❤

*▼ Pay special attention to your woman's breasts during foreplay as many women are very sensitive here. With a little imagination the attentive lover should find all sorts of ways to increase the intensity of her passion.*

# MASTURBATION

*Your body is a sensitive instrument, capable of giving you and your lover great pleasure. By exploring your feelings and responses yourself, both of you can gain an intimate knowledge of how to make that pleasure still more intense.*

What does the term 'masturbation' mean to you? For most of us, it is not only an embarrassing word but a taboo subject – something we never discuss, not even with our partner or our closest friends. But all of us would like to get more out of sex because of the pleasure it gives us, and first of all we have to know our own responses and what we like or do not like.

Pleasure is a combination of emotion and physical sensation, and this combination is different for each individual. The inhibitions we all feel about discussing what gives us sexual pleasure make it very difficult for us to say to our partner, 'I don't like this, this does nothing for me', particularly if we can't go on to say, '...but I do like this, this sensation is wonderful.'

### EXPLORATION AND DISCOVERY
It is much easier to steer your partner away from patterns of lovemaking which don't suit you if you can suggest an alternative. But don't forget that we can't expect anyone else to know what suits us if we don't know ourselves.

Touching our own bodies allows us to explore physical sensations in complete privacy and at our own speed. It helps us to become comfortable with our own bodies, to discover their immense capacity for sensual pleasure – a pleasure which we can then share with our lovers. Sadly, masturbation is often seen as a

second-rate substitute for sex. Of course it can be, but it is also an alternative to full intercourse as well as a useful learning tool, and it can be incorporated into your lovemaking to increase the pleasure and intimacy.

There are probably more old wives' tales about masturbation than any other

▼ *It's worth taking the time and making the effort to learn about yourself – the more you know about your body and how to give and receive pleasure from it, the better and more fulfilling your physical relationships will be.*

*I'VE LEARNED A LOT FROM WATCHING CLAIRE TOUCH HERSELF. NOW I KNOW WHAT SHE LIKES I CAN REALLY MAKE THE EARTH MOVE FOR HER – AND I FIND IT VERY EXCITING TO WATCH HER BRING HERSELF TO ORGASM.*

area of sexual activity. Little boys are told that it will lead to blindness, hair on the palms of the hands, impotence – the list goes on for ever. Little girls are given the impression that to acknowledge their sexuality is somehow 'not nice', that touching themselves 'down there' will spoil them for their husbands or turn them into sex addicts.

It doesn't do anything of the kind, of course, but over the years these false claims have given masturbation an extremely poor press. Even today, most people secretly feel that there is something 'wrong' about masturbation.

### WHO DOES IT?

Almost all men and women masturbate from time to time. It is said that 90 per cent of men admit to masturbating and the other 10 per cent are liars. Some people – including about a third of all women – say that they cannot remember a time in their lives when they have not masturbated. Others date its beginnings from puberty, while yet others seem to start when they are in a permanent relationship. But most of us begin at a very young age.

Almost all babies play with their genitals, and most parents are aware that their toddlers sometimes masturbate, although not to adult orgasm.

It is often thought that masturbation is less common among females than among males, but this is partly because it is easier for male children to find their sex organs and thus discover that playing with them is fun. Female masturbation is also more difficult to define.

With men, masturbation involves direct stimulation of the penis and generally ends in ejaculation. But for women, it is more complex. Every woman has her own preferences, and these may differ every time.

### WOMEN AND MASTURBATION

Almost any part of the female body can be a source of arousal and orgasm, and different kinds of caressing on different areas can give an infinite range of sensations – sensual as well as sexual and comforting as well as exciting.

There are also social reasons why some women do not practice obvious masturbation, but stimulate themselves in less apparent ways. Our parents tend to be much more tolerant of small boys holding their penises than of small girls touching themselves. However, by finding these 'no-hands' methods of stimulating themselves, girls can pretend they are not doing it.

Some little girls will masturbate when they are sitting on their heels or riding their bicycles. It can also be incorporated into

permissible contact, such as washing in the bath. In 20 years' clinical experience, one expert collected over one hundred indirect ways that women masturbate.

### FEELING GUILTY

Most definitions of masturbation infer that it ends in orgasm. So if it does not, a woman may think of herself as not masturbating. This kind of self-delusion is not confined to women. Some men are brought up to feel guilty or sinful about sex and, will also think of themselves as not masturbating. This is usually done either by rubbing the erect penis with no intention of ejaculating, or by blocking off the conscious knowledge of orgasm.

People who feel guilty may only

▼ *Women can make love to themselves in many ways, combining breast stimulation with stimulation of the clitoris, or even without using any direct genital contact at all.*

masturbate at the time between sleeping and waking, and so feel able to deny it because they are not fully conscious. These complex systems of denial indicate how guilty many people feel about arousing themselves sexually.

Yet masturbation is a valuable experience. It is the way most of us first learn about how our bodies respond to sexual stimulation. Just as we learn to talk before we hold a conversation, most of us masturbate before we learn to make love. Research shows that for many women, masturbation is the surest way to climax and that having learned how to reach orgasm in this way, they

> *IT'S COMFORTING BECAUSE THERE'S NO PRESSURE AND YOU DON'T FEEL YOU HAVE TO PERFORM. THERE'S NOBODY ELSE INVOLVED – YOU CAN JUST CONCENTRATE ON YOUR OWN PLEASURE.*

then transfer the knowledge into their sex life with their partners.

As well as learning about your own physical responses, masturbation is also an important part of learning that your body belongs first of all to yourself. Many women feel that their partners automatically have certain 'rights' and feel very uncomfortable about saying yes or no to sex, which can put a great deal of pressure on the relationship.

### WITHIN A PARTNERSHIP

However, masturbation is not something that stops once we start having sex. In fact, masturbation within a partnership is almost universal among men and very common in women, who often find that they can give themselves stronger orgasms than their partner can. Even so, many couples worry that it is only a second-class sexual pursuit.

In fact it has great value in its own right. If you are separated from your lover for a long time, or if one of you is unable to have sex – perhaps because of illness or surgery – masturbation can provide an answer which prevents either partner from having to look elsewhere for sex. And for times when one of you is not interested, there is a solution which does not threaten your partnership.

### POSITIVE ACTIONS

Masturbation and an active shared sex life are actually closely linked. Women who are in an enjoyable sexual relationship tend to masturbate more often than men in the same situation. Research has shown that women who masturbate a lot want sex more, not less.

Another way in which masturbation can be a positive force within a relationship is through the fantasies that are linked with it. We may well have committed ourselves to one person, but that doesn't mean we stop fancying anyone else. Masturbation is a good way of defusing the possible threat this might offer. When making love to ourselves, we can imagine we are with the person who has caught our eye, and keep any 'straying' within the bounds of fantasy.

### HOW MEN MASTURBATE

Most men, at least from their adolescence onwards, will stimulate the rim of the head of the penis by encircling it with their

*▼ ▶ For men, masturbation involves direct stimulation of the penis, either with the hand alone or by a closer simulation of full intercourse.*

fingers and then moving their hand up and down in a pumping action. This means that the thumb and index finger are 'vibrating' up and down against the rim, while the remaining fingers hold the shaft of the penis. The pressure used varies from man to man – some prefer a firm grip while others find a light touch more exciting. Some men use the other hand to stroke their scrotum, or other parts of their body.

Many men will pause at some stage to allow their arousal to build up, so that the pleasure is prolonged and the orgasm more intense. A variation on purely manual stimulation is to simulate sex by lying face down with the penis between the flat of the hand and the mattress and making thrusting movements.

middle finger, which is used to press the clitoris against the pubic bone. The pressure could be a direct pulsing on to the bone or a rubbing movement which increases in speed.

But this is only part of the range of stimulation open to women. Stroking the inner thighs, lower stomach, breasts

> *I'D NEVER TELL MY WIFE I MASTURBATE, I COULDN'T –*
> *I KNOW HOW MUCH TROUBLE IT WOULD CAUSE. SHE'D*
> *THINK I WAS SOMEHOW BETRAYING HER AND GET*
> *TERRIBLY UPSET, WHEN OF COURSE IT'S GOT NOTHING*
> *TO DO WITH THAT.*

The most usual way for women to masturbate is to lie on their backs and use one hand to stimulate the vulva. A few women will concentrate only on the vagina itself, inserting fingers or any roughly penis-shaped object, but most prefer clitoral stimulation. A common combination of movements might be to begin with light stroking of the pubis, with the fingers passing on either side of the clitoris on top of the outer lips. The pressure might then increase and the fingers close to squeeze the clitoris between them.

Direct clitoral stimulation can be made with a single fingertip, often the

and nipples can all be exciting. Some women find that pinching their nipples and then holding the pinch produces a slowly increasing surge of pleasure which helps them achieve orgasm.

It is often thought that women masturbate by inserting dildos or vibrators into their vagina, and that the bigger they are, the better. In fact, most women find this uncomfortable rather than arousing. Vibrators and dildos are mostly used to stimulate the clitoris, vaginal lips or nipples and women often do not insert anything inside the vagina. If they

| HOW OFTEN DO WOMEN MASTURBATE? | |
|---|---|
| **FREQUENCY** | **%** |
| ONCE A DAY OR MORE | 1 |
| NEARLY EVERY DAY | 4 |
| 1 TO 4 TIMES A WEEK | 25 |
| 1 TO 3 TIMES A MONTH | 23 |
| LESS THAN ONCE A MONTH | 47 |

| HOW OFTEN DO MEN MASTURBATE? | |
|---|---|
| **FREQUENCY** | **%** |
| ONCE A DAY OR MORE | 7 |
| NEARLY EVERY DAY | 12 |
| 1 TO 4 TIMES A WEEK | 46 |
| 1 TO 3 TIMES A MONTH | 17 |
| LESS THAN ONCE A MONTH | 18 |

◀ *Some women like very light pressure on the vulva; others may prefer a stronger touch. If you know your own preferences, both you and your partner can gain greater pleasure from your lovemaking.*

do, it is likely to be something less rigid than the hard plastic of most vibrators. They may also enjoy inserting something smaller into the anus and find that this intensifies their orgasm. Great care should be always be taken, though, as the rectal lining is very delicate and it is easy to spread germs from the bowel to the vagina. Do make sure anything you insert is clean and well lubricated.

### RUNNING WATER

Running water is very popularly used for clitoral stimulation. A jet of warm water from a showerhead, bidet or mixer tap directed over the clitoris is highly exciting for most women and can produce an intense orgasm.

Most women 'mix and match' different kinds of stimulation on different parts of their body, depending on how they feel.

Women can also have multiple orgasms during a single session, while men will usually stop masturbating after they have ejaculated.

### IF YOUR PARTNER MASTURBATES

Women are often very worried to find that their lover masturbates and take it as a sign that they are not 'enough' for him. This is why most men in a close relationship will masturbate behind locked doors, usually in the bathroom. But he will probably be doing it simply for the variety. Everyone likes a change and masturbation is something which produces another sensation and fits another mood.

Men are generally delighted at the thought of their partner making love to themselves. It takes a good deal of trust to bring up the subject with your partner, but once the initial embarrassment has been overcome, the act of masturbation can greatly increase the intimacy of a loving relationship. ❤

*21*

# SHARING MASTURBATION

*Many people think of masturbation as a solitary activity, but as a shared experience it can be one of the most exciting - and stimulating - ways a couple can learn about each other's needs and desires.*

Watching each other masturbate can be an ideal way of improving the quality of your lovemaking. By observing how your partner masturbates, you can learn how to bring them to orgasm in the ways they like best. It is also an ideal way to become totally at ease with each other.

First set the scene – ensure that the room you choose is private, warm and relaxing. If you find it relaxes you, perhaps have a little drink – not too much – beforehand. Use music too, if this helps to get the mood right. Have a bath or shower together, and then perhaps massage each other lovingly as you become aroused. Then take it in turns to teach each other what you like the most.

▶ *A woman's enjoyment of reaching a climax through masturbation can be a powerful turn-on for the male partner, as well as a rewarding guide to the timing and techniques that he can to bring into play when he next comes to stimulate her. Masturbation is far from a selfish experience.*

## WATCHING THE WOMAN

Masturbation can be tricky for many couples, because some women feel shy, and find it difficult to relax sufficiently in front of their partner to make themselves reach orgasm, even if they usually have them without any trouble.

The secret here is to start off by cuddling and setting the scene as before, then ask your partner to masturbate with the lights down low, or even off, while you hold her or caress her.

Slowly, over another session or two – and if she feels sufficiently relaxed – increase the light level as she becomes excited and oblivious to her surroundings. Then watch carefully what she does. You should note:

• her body and leg position
• what she does with both her hands
• where she puts her fingers to stimulate her vulva or clitoris
• the type, size and pressure of her hand movements, as these vary considerably in most women from stage to stage in their arousal sequence
• whether or not she puts fingers into her vagina
• if she stops stimulating herself and then restarts
• what facial, breast, vulval, clitoral and skin changes occur
• if she makes any noises or cries out during orgasm
• what she actually does at the moment of climax
• what changes occur as she calms down.

Now cuddle up and talk about the effect the experience had on you both – did you both find it pleasurable and helpful? Most men find watching their woman masturbating intensely arousing, possibly because it declares very powerfully that she is no innocent virgin, but a full-blooded, sexy woman.

*" AT FIRST I WAS REALLY SELF-CONSCIOUS ABOUT MASTURBATING IN FRONT OF MY BOYFRIEND BUT HE REALLY HELPED ME RELAX. IT ALSO HELPED HIM UNDERSTAND EXACTLY WHAT TURNS ME ON – AND IT REALLY SHOWS NOW WHEN WE'RE MAKING LOVE. "*

**I have heard some very strange things concerning masturbation – not least of which is that is can be damaging to health. Surely this can't be true?**

No, fortunately, masturbation is not harmful. In the last century, many doctors thought that masturbation had all kinds of serious effects. Today no doctor would give credence to such ideas. The only harm it can do is to your state of mind – if you feel guilty about it!

**I like using a vibrator on my clitoris because it gives me wonderful orgasms. Could this damage my ability to have orgasms in other ways?**

A vibrator is a very powerful stimulus and many women find that they experience their best orgasms in this way. However, it does not stop women being able to reach orgasm by using their own fingers, which is probably most women's preferred method.

# ATCHING THE MAN

Watching your man masturbate is a good way of finding out about his particular needs and desires. Cuddle him at the same time if he prefers and observe:

• the exact position of his hand
• the location of his fingers on his penis
• how much pressure he uses
• the rate, extent and type of movement
• the changes that occur in the penis, scrotum and testes
• other bodily changes, including his breathing rate, facial expression, muscle contractions, sweating and so on
• any other areas of the body he stimulates, for example his anus, the 'root' of his penis or his testes
• the amount of pre-ejaculatory secretion
• the size and force of the initial spurt of semen and the number, speed and force of further spurts
• the stage at which he stops stimulating himself
• the changes that occur as he calms down.

It is good idea to talk honestly about your experience. Learning all you can about his masturbation could take several sessions together.

respect are so variable compared with those of men.

No two individuals masturbate in the same way. This means that the 'teacher' must tell the 'pupil' exactly what he or she likes best. So make sure that you give specific, practical instructions – not just woolly generalizations. Put your partner's hands and fingers where you want them, and do not be shy or afraid to say what does not feel good.

After a certain amount of experience with one another, you will find that talk becomes unnecessary and communication will continue with hand movements, grunts, moans and other appreciative noises.

### FANTASIZE

Many people of both sexes find that if they rely on fantasies to turn them on during masturbation, then too much talking keeps them self-consciously aware of what is going on and so acts as a turn-off. So use these sessions to learn when it is time to stop talking and leave your partner to become abandoned to

Once you are at ease with watching each other masturbate and have learned all you can, you can make the most of mutual masturbation. No one knows by magic, or even after simply watching, how to stimulate their partner to orgasm. Even the most experienced man will have a lot to learn about his partner, if only because the needs of women in this

◀ *Masturbation is a good way of learning how our bodies respond to sexual stimulation.*

▲ *When you both feel confident about giving each other pleasure individually, it's time to try it together.*

▶ *Masturbating along with your partner is a sexy and stimulating way of learning how to bring him or her to orgasm.*

his or her individual erotic thoughts, fantasies and feelings.

Be aware of the whole body – many people enjoy having things done to them that do not involve their genitals. Many women, for example, like their breasts and nipples to be caressed or kissed and many men like to have their anus stimulated or their testes held or genitals squeezed. Simply concentrating on the penis or clitoris may not be enough and may actually desensitize your partner.

Be generous. Once you have settled down into your chosen position, you should aim to give your partner as much pleasure as possible. Do not go for the least possible you can get away with – go

for a really powerful, satisfying orgasm each time.

Some couples find it helpful to rate their orgasms out of ten so that they can chart their 'progress', and take note of the kind of stimulation they enjoy most.

Do what they like best. Once you know how best to excite your partner and to produce the best quality of orgasm for him or her, it is generally best to stick to whatever produces this on most occasions that you masturbate.

Most people like predictability in masturbation, and this is especially true of women. Many women say that they achieve their best orgasms whenever their man does exactly what they like the best every time. ❤

▲ *The moment of ejaculation can be an erotic event for both of you. Delaying the climax by taking a break in the middle of masturbating can sometimes give a man an intense orgasm.*

◀ *A good position for the man is to sit or kneel behind his partner, so that he has the freedom of movement to caress her breasts with one hand and stimulate her clitoris with the other. Kissing her neck and shoulders will only add to the fun!*

*HELPING EACH OTHER CLIMAX THROUGH MASTURBATION IS JUST AS PLEASURABLE AS PENETRATIVE SEX. WITH PRACTICE, YOU CAN TIME IT SO YOU BOTH COME TOGETHER – WHICH DOESN'T ALWAYS HAPPEN WITH OTHER FORMS OF LOVEMAKING.*

## LEARN THROUGH SHARING

AS WITH ANY LEARNING PROCESS, YOU MAY STUMBLE ONCE OR TWICE ALONG THE WAY. BUT HERE ARE SOME USEFUL TIPS WHICH WILL HELP YOU MASTER THE VARIOUS TECHNIQUES SUCCESSFULLY AND ENJOYABLY.

• GET IN THE MOOD. MAKE SURE THAT THE ROOM IS WARM, AND THERE IS NO CHANCE OF INTERRUPTION. A LITTLE MUSIC, SEXY READING MATTER OR VIDEOS ARE OPTIONAL EXTRAS THAT COULD HELP GET YOU BOTH AROUSED. HAVE A BATH TOGETHER, IF YOU WANT, AND CUDDLE EACH OTHER.

• GET COMFORTABLE. MASTURBATING EACH OTHER CAN BECOME TIRESOME IF YOU DO NOT GET THE POSITION RIGHT. AWKWARD, UNCOMFORTABLE BODIES DO NOT USUALLY FEEL SEXY. MAKE SURE THAT BOTH OF YOU ARE COMFORTABLE, AND THAT YOUR PARTNER'S GENITALS ARE AS CLOSE TO YOURS AS POSSIBLE TO HELP WITH MUTUAL STIMULATION.

• KEEP THE LIGHTS ON. YOU CANNOT LEARN MUCH IF YOU CANNOT SEE, SO IT IS A GOOD IDEA TO KEEP THE LIGHTS ON – PERHAPS DIMMED. AFTER ALL, WATCHING YOUR PARTNER CAN BE VERY EXCITING AND MANY WOMEN SAY THAT ONE OF THEIR GREATEST TURN-ONS IS WATCHING THEIR MAN CLIMAX.

• USE PLENTY OF LUBRICATION. DRYNESS IS A TURN-OFF. WHETHER THE MAN IS CARESSING HIS PARTNER'S CLITORIS OR SHE HIS PENIS, YOU MAY FIND THAT YOU NEED ADDED MOISTNESS. THE BEST AND SAFEST FORM OF LUBRICATION IS SALIVA – IT IS WARM AND ALWAYS AVAILABLE. ALTERNATIVES ARE KY JELLY OR BABY OIL BUT USE THEM SPARINGLY AS THEY CAN MAKE THINGS VERY STICKY AND UNCOMFORTABLE.

• A MAN CAN BE MASTURBATED USING TALC, BUT IT SHOULD NOT BE USED ON A WOMAN AS IT CAN CAUSE PROBLEMS IF IT FINDS ITS WAY UP INTO THE VAGINA.

# *I*MAGINATIVE FOREPLAY

*Familiarity can be a boon to good lovemaking, but, from time to time, it pays to vary your sexual routine and add a little magic to your love life.*

*T*he quality of foreplay can make or break a lovemaking session. Treat it perfunctorily and the sex can easily become ordinary and predictable. Pay attention to it and the experience becomes almost totally unique.

But before foreplay, making sex memorable for your partner involves deciding on what they want and like best and then putting it into action.

▼ *Men are more likely to be visually stimulated by the sight of a woman's body than the setting itself, so plan a lovemaking session around this and you cannot fail!*

## MAKING IT MEMORABLE FOR HER

Decide what atmosphere you wish to create. Women tend to be more influenced by the place in which they make love than are men. So if your partner loves romantic, candlelit evenings for two at home, prepare one for her, or if she likes making love in unusual places, do your best to accommodate her. If she likes flowers or small presents then give them to her. And if she likes you to dress in

*WHENEVER THE LOVEMAKING BECOMES A LITTLE TOO ROUTINE BETWEEN MY PARTNER AND ME, WE TRY AND RECALL THE ABANDONED LOVEMAKING WE INDULGED IN AS TEENAGERS. IT MAY NOT HAVE BEEN THE GREATEST SEX BUT IT WAS FULL OF FUN AND SPECIAL INTIMACY WHICH MAKES IT REALLY MEMORABLE FOR US.*

a particular way, then you should indulge her in her favorite fantasy.

Concentrate on giving her everything she wants during lovemaking. It is likely that when you first started making love with her, you were attentive and you listened to everything she said – and it is comparatively easy to re-create this behavior.

### MAKING IT MEMORABLE FOR HIM

Contrary to opinion, most men are no less influenced by mood when it comes to lovemaking. It is just that their sexual parameters are slightly different – they tend to be more visually stimulated by their partner. It is your body, and often the way you are dressed that can make sex memorable for him, so dress for him periodically. If he fancies you as a 'tart', dress and behave like one.

Tease him almost unmercifully. If you decide to wear no underwear, tell him that this is what you have done. Treat sex unselfishly, concentrating on making it memorable for him and, by so doing, memorable for yourself.

### ORGASM

Orgasm is generally the aim of lovemaking but often the most memorable sex can be achieved if you have nearly achieved orgasm only to subside and then be brought up to it again. But to avoid misunderstanding, it is a good idea to tell each other beforehand.

For the man who wants to bring his partner to the brink of orgasm, take time removing each of her garments, using your hands to run up and down her back, her legs and her stomach. Nibble her feet and calves and

▶ *You can bring your partner to the brink of orgasm using your hands or your mouth. If she raises her legs back towards her shoulders you can insert your fingers deeply into her vagina.*

behind her knees. Encourage her to stretch out and abandon herself to you.

When she is totally naked, use oil all over her but do not touch her breasts or vulva. Instead, lightly brush over them as you caress her less erogenous zones.

When you caress her breasts, pour oil onto them and knead it in. Then use the tip of your penis to trace a path around each nipple. If she tries to touch you, restrain her. Then use oil on her vulva with the other hand, first of all circling it before gently using a finger on her clitoris. When she is ready, insert as many fingers as she likes into her vagina and use the thumb of your hand on her clitoris. Do not let her come just yet.

## USING A VIBRATOR

A vibrator is one of the most versatile and variable sex aids for a woman. There are a number of ways you can use it on

▲ *Used creatively, a vibrator can give your partner exquisite sensations. Use it to massage the area around her genitals as well.*

*My wife still orgasms when we make love yet she says it lacks the old magic. What's wrong?*

*It sounds like you need to plan a return to courtship. Wine and dine your wife, appreciate her, buy her a small gift, communicate with her and pay attention to her. It is the sexual packaging that is at fault rather than the core of your sexuality. And all that is required from you is a little preparation and a desire to please.*

her, but for the purpose of making sex memorable do not use it to bring her to orgasm, only to the brink. Use it on her breasts and her buttocks as well as her vulva. If she likes it, insert the tip into her anus as well, although remember not to put it into her vagina afterwards as this may transfer anal bacteria.

Vary the speed setting as you alternate, using it inside her and on her clitoris. Make sure, as well, that you keep your

other hand busy all over her body. And don't forget to use your mouth too.

### HER – FOR HIM
Men love to be caressed and fussed over as much as women. The only difference is that, because they are more genitally orientated, they tend to require less time to become aroused. So although the quality of arousal should be memorable for him, it should not take too long, otherwise he will come too soon which may be fine for him but not so good for you.

Use your hands and your body to caress him. Trace a path along his back, from his feet to his neck, first with your hands and then your breasts.

Then turn him over and pour a little oil onto his stomach

▼ *Kissing should never be restricted to the mouth. Try kissing and caressing your partner all over – from the toes upwards. A slow and sensual build-up to foreplay will increase her pleasure in lovemaking tenfold.*

# CREATIVE LOVING

## THE RIGHT MOOD

THE BACK OF THE CAR, A DESERTED BEACH, OR THE COMFORT OF ONE'S OWN BEDROOM CAN ALL HAVE MAGICAL QUALITIES FOR SEX IF THE MOOD IS RIGHT. CREATING AN ATMOSPHERE AFTER A COUPLE HAS BEEN TOGETHER FOR SOME TIME NEEDS PREPARATION AND IMAGINATION – AND IT REQUIRES TIME.

LOVEMAKING IN A HURRY MAY BE FINE, BUT THE SENSATIONS THAT BRING US TO THE BRINK OF A UNIQUE ORGASM USUALLY DEMAND THAT TIME IS SPENT ON US – NOT JUST ON KISSING AND CARESSING, BUT ON THE WORDS WE USE TO EACH OTHER, AND THE SMALL LOOKS AND GLANCES WE EXCHANGE.

FAMILIARITY MAY BREED BETTER LOVEMAKING, TECHNICALLY, BUT PRE-SEXUAL FOREPLAY – THE PERIOD OF COURTSHIP SOMETIMES CALLED THE HONEYMOON PERIOD – IS SOMETHING THAT IS SADLY FORGOTTEN BY MANY COUPLES AFTER THEY HAVE BEEN TOGETHER FOR A WHILE.

▼ *Some women find it highly arousing when their partner kisses her perineum – the classic '69' position allows you to do this and also to stimulate her vulval area.*

and the tops of his legs. Rub it firmly in and then pour some more directly onto the tip of his penis and gently rub it in with both hands.

### PERFECT ORGASMS
A session of lovemaking may last anything from a few minutes to half an hour. But whatever lovemaking technique you choose, remember that it can always be changed if the mood changes. And orgasm may not necessarily be genitally induced – it could always be oral.

### THE WOMAN'S APPROACH
Mutual oral sex is highly erotic if your partner lies back on the bed and you squat over his mouth, facing away from him, and give him a full genital kiss on the lips using your vulva.

Lean slowly forward and rest on the bed with one elbow. Take the root of his penis into your mouth. Use long strokes, taking it as deeply into your mouth as you comfortably can and alternate this with licking the tip of his penis and sucking on it. All the time, remember to move your buttocks and direct his tongue onto your clitoris.

Remember that you are in control. Most men will find this position so highly arousing that if you increase the pace too much, he may come too soon. So do not be tempted to move your head too quickly or to suck too hard.

When you feel your own orgasm approaching, increase the momentum. Move your hand up and down his penis as you use your lips, tongue and mouth to bring him to orgasm.

### THE MAN'S APPROACH
Accept that from this position, the woman will control the pace of lovemaking and try to coincide your orgasm with hers. When she squats over your face use your tongue as creatively as you can. Start off by licking her clitoris and then try taking it between your lips and teeth and sucking on it. Be guided by what she wants. If you know she likes to have her perineum licked

*◀ During foreplay use your breasts as well as your hands all over his body. Most men will not fail to be aroused by this. Work your way down his body, then take his penis between your breasts.*

then do so. Do not keep your hands idle either. Use them to part her vaginal lips and pop your tongue inside her.

Transfer your fingers inside her – put in as many as she likes and use your tongue on her clitoris. Show that she is giving you pleasure by responding to the rhythm that she creates. Hold back your own orgasm until she comes.

### ANTICIPATING NEEDS

Remember that moods and needs can change during any individual session of lovemaking. The woman may suddenly want to take on a more dominant role, for example. Equally, the man may rel-

ish a change to a more aggressive or passive style of lovemaking after a while.

Good intercourse is all about rhythm and timing as well. The most determined thrusting can all be to no avail if the rhythm and timing are wrong.

All that is important – and the loving couple will recognize this – is that they are in tune with each other, and can anticipate each other's needs. ❤

*▼ You can change position a number of times in any one lovemaking session. If you want to try a rear-entry position, you are ideally placed to caress your partner's breasts.*

# ORAL SEX

*Oral sex offers a blend of intimacy, trust, generosity and tenderness which is often very different from intercourse, yet can produce a high level of excitement and be deeply satisfying.*

Oral sex has two different names. Kissing, licking and sucking the female sex organs is called cunnilingus. Similar mouth contact with the penis is called fellatio.

The simultaneous performing of fellatio and cunnilingus by two people to each other is known as *soixante neuf*, which is the French for 69. The numerals represent two people lying curled together head to toe.

Oral sex can be used as a complete sexual experience in itself with either or both partners being brought to orgasm. More often it is used as a part of foreplay before genital intercourse takes place.

For many women, cunnilingus is more exciting than intercourse. Lubrication is more readily provided by the mouth than the vagina and a man generally has more control over his mouth than his genitals.

The tongue, with its quick darting movements, is more tender than the skin of the fingers, and many women find that they have orgasms with oral stimulation even if they cannot do so in any other way.

For a man, fellatio is particularly exciting because it is so different from 'conventional' intercourse. The lips, lined as they are with tissues similar to the vagina itself, feel like a new vagina. It also shows a high degree of intimacy

▼ *Oral sex is a kiss that caresses the most intimate parts of your lover's body. It can add variety and inject new drive into the sex life of any couple.*

and it gives the man a chance to feel worshipped and play a passive role in bed, which he may welcome from time to time.

### IS ORAL SEX NORMAL?

Many people still find the mere thought of oral sex distasteful. They may think it is 'dirty' to use your lips and tongue on the organs used for urination. Or they may simply be shy.

Some men feel that any desire they have for oral sex is an expression of homosexual tendencies, about which they may feel afraid and ashamed.

For healthy couples, there is nothing perverted or unhygienic about oral sex. It is merely an extension of other forms of sexual activity. Most people kiss their partner's body when they have sex. Oral sex is a kiss that caresses the most intimate parts of your lover's body.

### NOTHING IS COMPULSORY

A problem can arise in a relationship when one partner wants oral sex and the other refuses. This can put real pressure on a relationship.

While being open and honest with each other about particular desires is positive in a relationship, no-one should be forced to do something they do not like. If you want oral sex and your partner does not, you should try to understand their reservations about it, and

explain them away with understanding and patience. But nobody should be made to feel obliged by the demands of emotional blackmail or the pleas of an inconsiderate lover. What a couple decide to do in bed is a matter of personal preference, and what feels right for both – not just one – of them at the same time.

▲ *The '69' position (soixante neuf) represents the supreme sexual sensation for some men, since they can give and receive pleasure simultaneously.*

> *I ALWAYS THOUGHT OF ORAL SEX AS A BIT DIRTY AND RATHER UNPLEASANT, BUT MY BOYFRIEND HELPED CHANGE MY MIND. SEX IS NOW THE BEST EVER, AND I REGULARLY HAVE ORGASMS.*

### PLAY IT SAFE

• YOU CAN CONTRACT AIDS IF YOU HAVE ORAL SEX WITH A PERSON WHO IS HIV POSITIVE, SO PRACTICE SAFE SEX AND USE A CONDOM. A MAN SHOULD NOT PERFORM CUNNILIGUS ('GO DOWN') ON HIS PARTNER UNLESS HE IS ABSOLUTELY CERTAIN OF HER SEXUAL HISTORY OR UNLESS THEY HAVE BEEN IN A LONG-TERM MONOGAMOUS RELATIONSHIP.

• DON'T BRUSH YOUR TEETH IMMEDIATELY BEFORE OR AFTER ORAL SEX AS MINOR ABRASIONS CAUSED BY OVERZEALOUS BRUSHING, A HARD TOOTHBRUSH OR BLEEDING GUMS PROVIDE AN IDEAL ROUTE FOR THE SPREAD OF INFECTIONS OF ALL TYPES.

# *H*ER FOR HIM

*◄ Oral sex should be a
mutual pleasure, so
choose a position
which is comfortable
for both partners.
A good position
for fellatio is
with the man
standing and
the woman
kneeling in
front of him.*

Although it is often thought that a women kisses and sucks a man's penis because it is so pleasant for him, many women do it because it gives them such intense sensations.

The idea behind fellating a man is to see it as a form of intercourse and treat it accordingly. No-one would dash into sex without foreplay and it is the same when fellating a man. Tease him and caress him in non-genital ways first and then slowly arouse him in the ways that you know work best.

Men tend to be much more predictable in what they like than are women, and what excites one man will almost certainly excite another. All the man has to do is to tell his lover of any likes and dislikes.

The only preparation necessary for fellatio is for the man to make sure that his genitals are clean.

### HOW TO FELLATE A MAN
Once the ground rules are set and foreplay is well under way, find a position in

## DOs AND DON'TS

DON'T BITE THE GENITALS, HOWEVER PLAYFULLY. IN THE HEAT OF THE MOMENT IT IS EASY TO GET CARRIED AWAY AND HURT YOUR PARTNER.

DO BE SCRUPULOUSLY CLEAN. WASH YOUR GENITALS EVERY DAY.

DO BE CAREFUL. A SUDDEN THRUST OF THE PENIS DEEP INTO A WOMAN'S MOUTH IS NOT ONLY INCONSIDERATE, IT CAN BE DANGEROUS.

DON'T EVER BLOW DOWN THE GENITALS. IT CAN ACTUALLY KILL A WOMAN BY FORCING AIR UP HER UTERUS AND INTO HER BLOODSTREAM. IT CAN ALSO BE DANGEROUS FOR A MAN.

◄ *Fellatio is a good way to re-arouse a man for a second round of love-making. A woman who genuinely wants to fellate her lover – either because she wants to give him exquisite pleasure or herself powerful sensations – will be able to produce an erection in all but the most stubborn penis.*

which you can really savor and enjoy your lover's penis. Positions can vary. Some men prefer to lie back in bed, others prefer to sit down. A good position is for the man to stand with his hands on his hips and his erect penis at your face level. You can then kneel before him, leaving your hands free to caress him and play with his testicles and anus.

Next, take his penis into the palm of your hand and, keeping your teeth out of the way, moisten the head with saliva. Then put the head of the penis into your mouth as far as is comfortable and move your head so that the penis goes in and out. The secret is to keep the teeth well out of the way at all times.

Once the man is sighing with pleasure at all this, you can remove the penis from your mouth and run the tongue up and down the length of the organ and tease his testicles too. This drives most men wild, as does running and flicking the tongue over the frenulum, the little ridge of skin on the underside of the penis. After a few minutes' stimulation, stop and tease him by turning your attention elsewhere on his body – nibbling him, and kissing him all over.

Return to the penis and put it firmly into your mouth, squeezing his testicles gently at the same time if he likes it. Be guided by the man as to how much in and out movement he likes.

Swirl your tongue around the head of the penis so that you never lose contact with it. Do this clockwise and then anti-clockwise. Dart your tongue into and out of the slit in the end of his penis and then continue swirling combined with the in and out movements. During all of this, make use of your hands too – ensure that you are giving your partner ecstatic sensations.

If you have decided not to take the

▼ *On certain occasions – such as after childbirth or when contraception is unavailable – oral sex can be the most practical way to make love. It produces a very different but equally high level of excitement and satisfaction.*

semen into your mouth, as he hardens finally, take the penis out of your mouth and masturbate him so that he comes over your breasts. Do not try for vaginal penetration at this stage – it rarely works well if a man is just about to come.

Many couples do not take fellatio to the extent of ejaculation, but use it as a form of foreplay soon to be followed by intercourse.

The secret here is to get to know your man's unique signs of arrival at the pre-ejaculatory stage by watching for muscle tension, breathing changes, noises and any movements he makes as he is getting close to orgasm.

If necessary, squeeze the head of his penis between your finger and thumb so as to cool him off for a while, until you are ready to be penetrated.

# HIM FOR HER

Performing cunnilingus successfully is much more difficult than performing fellatio. Almost all men will become erect and come quickly with adequate oral sexual attention from a woman. For women things can be very different, mainly because individual women are so variable in their sexual needs and genital pleasures.

As with fellatio, the only prerequisite is cleanliness of the sex organs. Washing immediately beforehand, however, is unnecessary. Ordinary daily bathing is enough.

Put a pillow under the woman's bottom to raise her pubic area to make it more comfortable for both of you, and then nuzzle her all over and kiss her breasts and nipples. Tease her by running your lips over sensitive parts of her body but do not tickle, as this could be more irritating than pleasurable.

Nuzzle into her vulva and kiss all around the area. Kiss her large lips and run your tongue along the length of them. Take one in between your lips and suck it. Suck the inner lips gently in this way as well.

Lick around the vaginal opening and the area between the vagina and the

▲ *This position puts the woman in control of her orgasm during cunnilingus. She presses her vulva down on her lover's mouth and brings herself to orgasm at her own pace.*

## DID YOU KNOW?

ORAL SEX HAS BEEN PRACTICED BY MEN AND WOMEN FOR THOUSANDS OF YEARS. THE EGYPTIANS WERE PARTICULARLY KEEN ON IT – EGYPTIAN WHORES WORE LIPSTICK TO ADVERTIZE THE FACT THEY COULD FELLATE A MAN. CLEOPATRA IS SAID TO HAVE BEEN THE MOST CELEBRATED OF ALL ITS EXPONENTS. SHE WAS CALLED 'GAPER' BY THE GREEKS AND IS SAID TO HAVE FELLATED A HUNDRED ROMAN SOLDIERS IN A SINGLE NIGHT.

FURTHER EAST, ANTHER ORAL SEX LEGEND INVOLVES WU HU, AN EMPRESS OF THE T'ANG DYNASTY. IN AN ATTEMPT TO ELEVATE HER OWN STATUS AND BE IN A POSITION OF DOMINANCE OVER MEN, SHE IS SAID TO HAVE INSISTED THAT ALL VISITING GOVERNMENT AND FOREIGN OFFICIALS SHOULD PAY HOMAGE BY PERFORMING CUNNILINGUS ON HER.

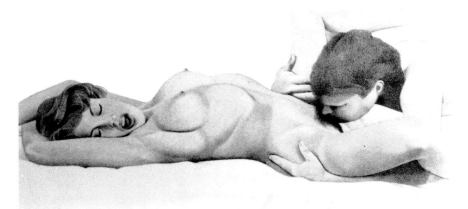

*◀ One of the most comfortable ways for a woman to enjoy oral sex is to lie back with her legs apart, leaving her partner free to use his tongue to explore her most sensitive areas.*

anus. Poke your tongue into her vagina and pop it in and out. As she becomes highly aroused and her vaginal juices start to flow, transfer your attention to the clitoris.

What you do to this sensitive organ should be dictated by what your partner most enjoys. Lick all around the area, but go gently on the tip itself as this can be exquisitely sensitive.

Some do not like the actual clitoris licked at all, while others enjoy very firm sucking and tonguing as they near their climax. As she becomes even more

aroused, put a couple of fingers inside her vagina.

From time to time stop the oral caressing and concentrate your hands on her vagina and other parts of her body. This will please her and produce different sexual sensations. ♥

*▼ By lavishing kisses and caresses on every part of a woman's body and not just her genitals during oral sex, a man can heighten and prolong his lover's excitement and pleasure.*

# INTIMATE KISSING

*Within a loving relationship, oral sex can be an integral part of a couple's sexual repertoire and most women find it a gentle yet highly arousing form of lovemaking.*

A man's mouth can be highly erotic and arousing when used in the right way on almost any part of a woman's body. In reality, oral sex includes the kissing and sucking of any part of her body – unfortunately most people concentrate on the genitals to the exclusion of other oral pleasures.

Almost all women enjoy oral sex that does not involve the genitals. They see it as romantic as it shows how much their man loves them. But when it comes to having their genitals kissed, licked and sucked, things can be rather different.

Some women see this as the most intimate thing a man can do to – and for – them and so greatly value it as a sign of his total love. Others think of their genitals as dirty and naughty and they cannot imagine anyone liking them, let alone wanting to kiss them.

At least some of these women can be persuaded to change their minds if, once they are aroused by clitoral or other stimulation, the man gently but firmly

▲ *For many women oral sex can be an exciting part of lovemaking, either as a prelude to intercourse or as an arousing alternative to penetrative sex.*

starts to kiss first around the vulval area and then the clitoris. Be careful not to tickle and make every effort to reproduce with your tongue what your partner usually does herself during masturbation and you will soon overcome her inhibitions.

### NON-GENITAL ORAL SEX

Lie alongside your partner face to face. Kiss her face gently all over, not forgetting to suck her ear lobes, if she likes it. Kiss her mouth, lips and tongue and arouse her further by caressing her body with your hands. The beauty of almost all the oral sex positions is that they leave the hands free to caress and arouse other parts of the woman's body.

Move down her body so that your head is on a level with her breasts. From here you can kiss her breasts, suck her nipples, put the whole of a breast into your mouth or blow on her nipples.

Run your tongue around her nipples and probe deeply with it into her breasts under the nipple and areola. Never bite, except very gently, and then not as she climaxes as you could do damage because she will be less sensitive to pain then.

This will all be especially arousing to

*Oral sex has always been an important part of our lovemaking. But since coming off the Pill my periods are very long. Neither one of us wants to wait, so is there anything we can do?*

*Yes. You can either use a tampon, with the string tucked in, or a cap (diaphragm) and wash thoroughly. But most importantly, remember that this advice applies only to partners who are faithful to one another and are totally secure about each other's sexual history.*

the breast-centerd woman. It is a good position for using during a period or in pregnancy. Some women have an orgasm when this much time and care is taken to arouse their breasts.

### TRAVEL DOWNWARDS

Now move your mouth down onto her stomach. Lick and kiss her navel and run your mouth and lips all over her stomach, round and round in circles. Work down towards her vulva but, at this stage, do not touch it with either your hands or your mouth.

▼ *If the man places his hands under his partner's buttocks as she lies back on the bed, he can raise her body slightly to get her vulva at a level where he can kiss, suck or lick the whole area.*

◀ *If the man lies on his back with his partner sitting astride his head he can use his tongue to penetrate deep into her vagina. Many women find positions such as this one very arousing as they are free to move their body to enhance sexual sensation.*

Lie in between your partner's feet, perhaps kneeling on the floor at the end of the bed. You can now kiss and suck her toes and feet. Some women so enjoy this that they nearly have a climax, even if the rest of their body is not touched. This is a good position for the woman who likes to caress her own breasts and/or clitoris while her partner caresses her feet orally.

Do not forget her hands. Get into any

▼ *If the woman reclines on a comfortable chair well propped up with cushions, she is at an ideal height for her kneeling partner to stimulate her clitoris with his tongue.*

position you find comfortable and take her hand in yours or lie it, back downwards, on the bed. Run your tongue all over it and between the fingers and then suck her fingertips and kiss her palm, caressing it with your tongue.

# VARIATIONS

Once your partner has been aroused by non-genital oral contact, she will probably be very receptive to genital oral contact. This is the best time to try, but go gently if she has any qualms about oral sex. The best position is probably with the woman lying flat on her back with her legs apart. The man lies in between her legs so that he can easily lick, kiss and suck any part of her genitals. A major problem with this is neckache, so prevent this by putting

## TIPS FOR ORAL SEX

FOR HIM:
• SHAVE – DESIGNER STUBBLE WILL ONLY SCRATCH THE DELICATE SKIN AROUND AND INSIDE YOUR PARTNER'S GENITALS.
• SUCK, DON'T BITE, THE CLITORIS.
FOR HER:
• WASH YOUR VULVA, PERINEAL AND ANAL AREAS THOROUGHLY.
• LEAVE OFF YOUR PANTIES OR WEAR OPEN-CROTCH PANTIES SO THAT YOU WILL BE ABLE TO GET DOWN TO THINGS EASILY.
FOR BOTH:
• ONLY HAVE ORAL SEX IF YOU ARE FAITHFUL TO EACH OTHER AND ARE SURE ABOUT EACH OTHER'S SEXUAL HISTORY.

a pillow or two (depending on how saggy your bed is) under her hips. This will raise the vagina and bring it into a good position.

This position is good for licking and kissing the clitoris but less so for putting the tongue in the vagina or caressing the perineum or anus.

A good variation of this position is for the woman to lie in the same way, but for the man to turn around to face her feet. He now has his genitals over her face and she can suck and kiss his penis if that is what they both enjoy. If not, he can angle his body so that she does not have his genitals in her face.

By supporting himself on his elbows, he can kiss her vulva and clitoris very easily. The main precaution here is to be sure not to put too much weight on the woman's

▶ *A fun position for the really adventurous and supple couple. The woman lies with her legs in the air, taking most of her weight on her shoulders and gripping her partner's legs for support. He leans over, legs slightly bent, and kisses or licks her vulval area and her perineum.*

*I don't like the idea of oral sex as I am sure that I must smell unpleasant in this area. Do you think I should use a vaginal deodorant?*

*Certainly not. This problem is more likely in your mind as you believe your genitals are dirty. If you wash before you go to bed, there is absolutely no reason why your genitals should smell.*

*▲ The woman supports her weight on her arms and her toes, aided by her partner who places one hand under her buttocks. Her partner is now ideally placed to caress her vulval area with his tongue.*

body. It should all be on the man's knees and elbows. In this position the man can reach under his partner's thighs, pull them apart, and open the outer lips so as to give the best possible access for oral sex. The skillful man can even insert the fingers of one hand (or both) into the vagina while kissing the clitoris and the vulval area. This is also an excellent position for the couple who like to use a dildo or vibrator in the woman's vagina while she is being caressed orally. The man can watch it going in and out and the woman's hands are free to caress him and she can suck

his penis if she wants to.

The woman lies with her hips on the edge of the bed and her feet flat on the floor. The man kneels between her thighs and kisses and rubs her vulva and clitoris. As she becomes more excited the woman can pull her

▼ *This is another position that allows freedom of movement for the woman while being relaxing for the man. The man can also caress his partner's buttocks, open up her vulval area and pay close attention to her clitoris, vagina and perineum.*

thighs back to her chest, but still keeping them apart so that he has access to her open vulva. This is an exceptionally good position for the woman who likes her man to insert his tongue into her vagina.

All of this can be repeated with the woman lying on a table. This is in many ways more comfortable for the man because he has to bend down less as the woman's vulva is more level with his face.

The man lies flat on his back and the woman kneels over his chest and gives him her vulva to kiss. She can also orally caress his penis.

The man kneels down in front of the woman who stands, feet wide apart. He can now lick, kiss and suck her vulva underneath. This can be fun if the woman is fully dressed, apart from her panties. He is then covered by her skirt.

Finally, for the adventurous couple, the man lies down on his back on the bed or the floor with his knees drawn up. The woman now kneels over his face, legs wide apart, facing him, with her vulva over his mouth. She then leans backwards on to his knees and relaxes with her head over his knees. The vulva is exceptionally wide open and the man can push his tongue into her vagina and caress her vulva and clitoris with his mouth. ❤

*TO ME, THERE'S NO BETTER WAY TO MAKE A WOMAN FEEL ADORED THAN IF HER MAN GIVES HER LONG AND LINGERING ORAL SEX – AND OBVIOUSLY LOVES IT.*

*When kissing my wife's vulva I find I can't get down enough to get my tongue into her vagina. What can I do?*

*The anatomy of some women makes this very difficult. But you could try putting her hips on a pillow and then when you have your face near her vulva you can push your hands under her bottom and lift up her hips more. If she is highly aroused and ready for your caress she'll pull her thighs back and this will arch her bottom up even more. This should give you all the access you need.*

45

# 2

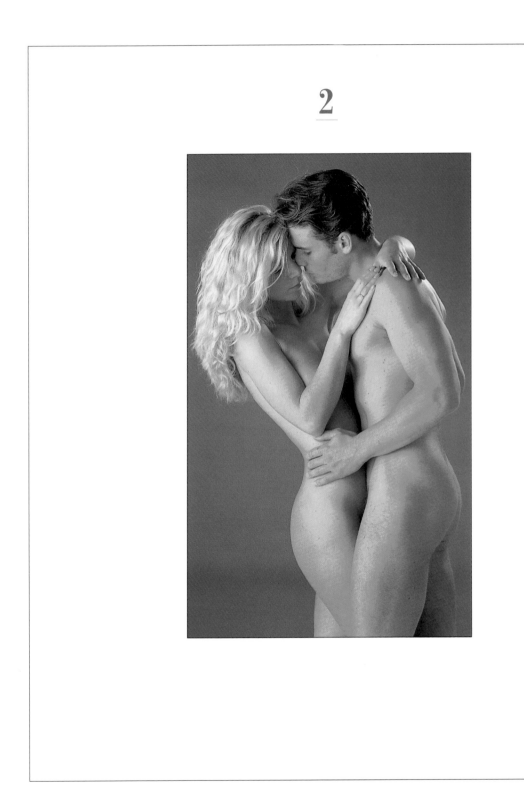

# Loving Positions

There is always something new to be discovered in the act of love. The Ancient Chinese masters believed that lovemaking should be a unique experience every time. This may be a tall order for most of us, but many couples would probably enjoy expanding their sexual repertoire when the mood is right. The human sexual response is so full of variety that sex can be as exciting and innovative, or as reassuringly predictable, as you like. In this chapter you will find adventurous ideas, some with the man in the dominant role, others with the woman most active.

# WOMAN ON TOP

*If you want sensational lovemaking, reverse the traditional roles and let the woman take the initiative. From the wildly erotic to the athletic, the variety of possibilities and positions makes sex electric!*

For the woman who likes to take the initiative and the man who enjoys watching his partner as they make love, woman-on-top positions cannot be beaten. And with deep penetration as an added bonus, they can can increase the sexual pleasure for both partners in any loving relationship by adding new sensations to your lovemaking.

Almost all men say that, on some occasions at least, they like to have the initiative taken away from them and, just as some women feel flattered to be taken with great ardor, so it is also true that many men like to be 'taken' by their female partner in this way.

### INCREASING AROUSAL

Before penetration, it can be fun for both if the woman teases a little. She can hold her lover's penis firmly, masturbating him while touching her vagina with the tip of it. She can also use it to stimulate her clitoris and her vaginal lips. before actual penetration. Play this game until neither of you can, nor wants to, hold back any longer.

Control is one of the first reasons women give when stating

▼ *In this position, the woman is free to move as she feels, while the man can run his hands over the full length of her body. This way, both partners can watch each other's pleasure.*

a preference for the woman-on-top position. Once the penis enters the vagina, the woman is in control of it in a way she cannot ever be when being penetrated in any other way.

### ANGLE AND RHYTHM

Once in position, the woman can change the angle and rhythm of penetration as she pleases, by rocking backwards and forwards and from side to side, swivelling her pelvis or moving up and down.

She can also lean forward to kiss her lover, sit up while he runs his hands over her body, reach to stroke his scrotum or anus or lean back to let his penis push against her G spot on the front wall of her vagina.

But most importantly she can alter the depth of penetration to suit herself and her lover.

### GENTLE MOVEMENTS

Many women find that if they are in a position where they are leaning backwards, they can only move their hips very slightly. But small, rythmic movements of the pelvis can give you both entirely different sensations. The temptation to continue in a thrusting motion is a strong one, but slow, gentle movements in this position can prolong the lovemaking and lead to a deeply satisfying climax for both

It is very easy to

stimulate the woman's clitoris in this position. The woman can squat or lie to bring it into contact with the man's pubic bone and then move her hips to rub against him, or it can be slowly and carefully caressed by hand.

▲ *Control the depth and rhythm of penetration by facing away from your partner.*

"*IT WASN'T UNTIL WE MADE LOVE IN THE WOMAN-ON-TOP POSITION THAT I WAS ABLE TO HAVE AN ORGASM WITH DAVID INSIDE ME. THIS WAY, HE COULD STIMULATE MY CLITORIS WITH THE SHAFT OF HIS PENIS.*"

◀ *Here, the woman can move her hips freely to control the depth of penetration, and hold her lover's head close against her breasts. It is a close and loving position with surprising scope for movement by the woman.*

and then circles her hips around the base instead of using sliding movements up and down the shaft, there should not be a problem.

### FACING AWAY

The other basic position is for the woman to kneel astride the man's penis, but facing away from him. This offers deep penetration and allows him to caress her back, the lower region of her body and her anus. He can watch his penis going in and out of her, especially if she leans forward, and she can stimulate her clitoris with one hand.

Facing away from the man can be as sensuous as facing towards him, as in this position the woman can caress his testicles and inner

# TOP POSITIONS

The basic woman-on-top position begins with the man lying flat on his back. The woman kneels astride his body, facing his head, and gently guides his penis inside herself. By moving her body up and down she can control both the speed and depth of penetration and her hands are free to caress him. He can handle her body and breasts and he can see his penis going into her.

From this position, the woman can lean forwards so that her breasts rest on her lover's chest or over his face. This reduces the range of her movement, but she can still raise and lower her hips over the penis while her partner is able to bury his face between her breasts and lick and suck her nipples.

It can be easy for the man's penis to slip out of the woman when she leans forward in this way. However, if she keeps her movements small and shallow, or simply presses herself firmly down on his penis

▼ *This one requires strong leg muscles and you will not be able to hold it for long, but it does give very deep penetration.*

thighs. The atheletic can swivel around from a facing position on his erect penis. This can be a whole new pleasure for both.

When the woman is facing away the man, can touch and squeeze the full curve of her buttocks and run his fingers over and around her anus.

### HIGHLY EROTIC

Many men find it highly erotic to watch themselves entering the woman, and of course this position offers the perfect view. It is also good for deep penetration and for stimulating the female G spot, which is on the front wall of the vagina.

Of course, in this position the couple cannot watch each other's facial reactions, and the man cannot always handle the woman's breasts during lovemaking. But this need

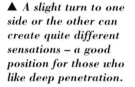

▲ *A slight turn to one side or the other can create quite different sensations – a good position for those who like deep penetration.*

not be a disadvantage for a couple, it is simply a matter of choosing to experience different sensations for different times and moods.

In either of the basic woman-on-top positions – woman facing man, woman facing away – there are delightful variations. The woman can kneel, squat or sit with her legs out straight. If she

▲ *Most men love the rich curves of a woman's bottom and this is one way to appreciate them to the full while also watching their penis going into their lover.*

wants the sensation of more contact, she can lie stretched out on top of the man and feel his skin along the full length of her body.

She can also sit sideways on her lover's penis and bring his leg up between hers and towards her chest. This is a particularly good position for couples who enjoy the sensation of deep penetration.

### WATCHING AND LISTENING

As always when making love, take care to watch or listen to your lover's reactions. This way you will quickly find out what pleases each of you and how you can best work to increase each other's pleasure, arousal and satisfaction.

If her lover is uncircumcised, she can gently push back his foreskin as far as it will go and then move up and down on the exposed head of his penis. This is easier from a squatting position, which is tiring to hold but it gives a man intense pleasure and can make him come very quickly. Penetration is obviously quite shallow, so this may be less exciting for the couple.

For deep penetration, another idea is for her to take him fully inside her and then pulse her fingertips fast against the base of his penis, with the heel of her hand resting on her lower stomach. If she positions her fingers so that they vibrate her clitoris at the same time, it can be intensely exciting for both.

In many lovemaking positions, the woman's movements are restricted. Most woman-on-top positions, however, offer her more freedom to move as she pleases. She can even change positions mid-way through the lovemaking, keeping her partner's penis inside her

# MAKING IT LAST

If the man does not want to come too quickly, woman-on-top positions are good for practicing delayed ejaculation – especially useful for men who sometimes suffer from premature ejaculation.

A man's erection and ejaculation reflexes are slowed down when he is on his back and there is time to use

▼ *Simply turning around on his penis opens a new range of possibilities. If the woman is shy about touching her clitoris while he is watching, this position can make it easier for her and she can gently caress his scrotum at the same time.*

the special 'squeeze technique' of preventing ejaculation. If he feels he is coming too soon, he can signal to the woman who can take his penis out and squeeze the top of the glans firmly between her fingers until he begins to lose his erection. She can then re-arouse him and they can continue making love.

# ℙREGNANCY

Woman-on-top positions are ideal during pregnancy. There is no pressure on the woman's stomach and it is easy for her to make sure that the depth and the speed of penetration are comfortable. The man can see and touch her new, full shape, and this kind of gentle, tender lovemaking can be highly arousing for both partners. In this way, intercourse can be possible almost entirely throughout the pregnancy.

Woman-on-top positions are also useful if the man is recovering from a serious illness or surgery, or the woman has recently given birth, because the woman can relax, knowing that her partner will not overdo things.

It is also important to remember that everyone is built differently. Some women's genitals are set very much more forward

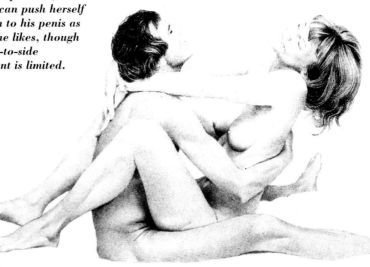

▶ *In this position, the woman can push herself down on to his penis as far as she likes, though her side-to-side movement is limited.*

▼ *Making love with the woman on top allows you to use your imagination in a variety of positions. You can also enjoy some really erotic foreplay.*

than others. This brings the penis into contact with the clitoris in a different way and means that deep penetration for one couple will be shallow for another. As with all sex positions, experimentation is the key, and with a little imagination you will soon find out what suits you both.

# MAN ON TOP

*Lovemaking positions where the man is on top are not always passive for the woman. With many of them, the woman can control the degree of penetration and dictate the pace of intercourse.*

For many couples, the most popular position in which to make love is the so-called 'missionary position' in which the woman lies on her back with her legs open as she is penetrated by the man who lies on top of her. This is the basic model of all man-on-top positions – all the others tend to be variations on the same theme.

### TOPS WITH LOVERS
The missionary position is the most popular lovemaking position for many reasons. Many women consider it the most romantic position, almost certainly because the couple are always face to face. Every expression can be noticed, they are free to kiss and each partner can see that they are being loved – something that is not possible in some other positions, such as the rear-entry ones.

The missionary position, being such a passive one for the woman, absolves her of the responsibility of making anything much happen. Some women can relax and enjoy lovemaking more if they do not take the dominant, active role.

Closely allied to such feelings in the woman are parallel, but opposite feelings in the man. Some men enjoy 'domi-

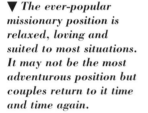

▼ *The ever-popular missionary position is relaxed, loving and suited to most situations. It may not be the most adventurous position but couples return to it time and time again.*

*◀ Kissing is an important, but often neglected, part of lovemaking. Man-on-top positions give a couple the perfect opportunity to kiss and caress, thereby creating an even greater sense of intimacy.*

nating' their partner during intercourse, and tend most to enjoy such positions – although from time to time, most men enjoy other positions in which their partner takes the lead and control.

Many women experience great pleasure from being dominated during intercourse. Such women enjoy sex particularly if the man is in control and makes everything happen. The missionary position is ideal for this. The man, being on top, controls the thrusting and can pin the woman down to the bed and take her roughly and at his pace.

Being 'taken' like this can be highly exciting to some women. For the woman who is at all guilty about her sexual needs and appetites, this position leaves her free of guilt, because she can think of herself as being overpowered by a much stronger man.

### FREE TO KISS

Because the couple's faces are close together, they can easily kiss – not just lips but all over each other's faces and even breasts and necks. This helps create a loving and caring atmosphere. For the woman who is aroused by nipple

*▼ The simple missionary position is ideal for couples who want to make love gently. When deep penetration is painful – for example, after a woman has had a baby – then this is the position to choose.*

stimulation, the man-on-top position allows the man to kiss her nipples.

By altering the angle of her thighs to her chest, the woman can change the degree of penetration even if the man stays in exactly the same position. As she brings her knees nearer to her chest, the penis goes in deeper. The woman can find just the right angle to give her the best sensations – perhaps as her lover stimulates her cervix with the tip of his penis. A variation of this is for the woman to rock her pelvis backwards and forwards. If, at the same time, she 'milks' her partner's penis by contracting and relaxing her pelvic muscles, this can be extremely exciting for him.

## BEST FOR BABIES!

The man-on-top positions are very good for couples who are trying to have a baby, because penetration can be very deep. If the woman holds onto her legs behind her knees and draws her thighs right back, sperm can be deposited deep in the vagina – at the neck of the womb. This provides the best chance of conception occurring.

If the woman stays lying down after sex, with a pillow under her hips, the semen stands the best possible chance of entering her cervix and the sperm will then be able to fertilize an egg.

## MORE THAN JUST ROMANTIC

Because it is a romantic yet fairly unadventurous position, it is a

▼ *By supporting his weight on his hands the man can control the depth of penetration as he thrusts in and out.*

## THE JOY OF BEING A CAT LOVER

AN AMERICAN PSYCHOTHERAPIST HAS COME UP WITH A REVOLUTIONARY VARIATION ON THE MISSIONARY POSITION THAT PROMISES TO HELP MORE WOMEN REACH ORGASM DURING INTERCOURSE – AND EVEN MAKE SIMULTANEOUS ORGASM A REALITY FOR MANY COUPLES. THIS BREAKTHROUGH, CALLED THE COITAL ALIGNMENT TECHNIQUE OR CAT FOR SHORT, WORKS BY ENSURING THAT THE CLITORIS GETS THE KIND OF CONTINUOUS STIMULATION NECESSARY FOR ORGASM. RATHER THAN MAKING SENSATION DEPENDENT ON FRICTION FROM IN-AND-OUT THRUSTING, CAT RELIES ON KEEPING CONSTANT CONTACT BETWEEN THE PENIS AND THE CLITORIS DURING LOVEMAKING. POSITION IS ALL IMPORTANT. THE MAN LIES ON TOP OF THE WOMAN WITH HIS PELVIS OVERRIDING HERS, SO THAT THE SHAFT OF HIS PENIS PRESSES AGAINST HER MONS VENERIS. MOVEMENT HAS TO BE RHYTHMIC AND IDENTICAL IN PACE AND PATTERN. THE WOMAN STARTS BY PRESSING UPWARDS, FORCING HER PARTNER'S PELVIS BACKWARDS, WHILE HE USES RESISTANCE TO PROVIDE COUNTERPRESSURE AGAINST HER CLITORIS. ON THIS UPWARD STROKE, THE WOMAN'S VAGINA ENGULFS THE MAN'S PENIS MORE DEEPLY. AS THE MAN'S PELVIS MOVES DOWNWARDS, THE WOMAN'S PELVIS IS FORCED BACKWARDS AND SHE PROVIDES THE COUNTERPRESSURE. FOR BEST RESULTS PRESSURE MUST BE CONSTANT, STEADY AND RHYTHMIC.

▲ *If the woman lies on her side and raises her upper leg, the man can then cuddle into the front of her body and penetrate her. Most couples find this a particularly loving way to have intercourse.*

particularly good one when having sex with a new partner. While you are still learning about one another, it makes sense to go for a position that is non-threatening and loving.

It allows a couple to kiss and caress. The woman's hands are free to caress the man. This could be especially valuable – showing him that he is loved and wanted in the new relationship. The missionary position lays neither partner open to strangeness, anxiety and unfamiliarity.

Because the man has control of the thrusting he can control his speed to orgasm. This is good news for the individual who fears losing control of ejaculation. A 'trigger-happy' man can thus stop when he feels ejaculation approaching, and a man who needs a great deal of thrusting to maintain his erection will also benefit.

▼ *In this position, known as the 'Rutting Deer', the degree of penetration is controlled by the position of the woman's legs.*

# VARIATIONS

The *Kama Sutra* and Chinese pillow books list many variations on the 'missionary' position. Often the difference is in slight detail only, but there are many other simple, man-on-top positions that can be tried for a change.

• The missionary position with one of the woman's legs pulled back to her chest is a pleasant variation that skews the woman's pelvis and enables the man to stimulate her ovary on one side. This may be tender for some women, so the man should be careful.

• The man kneels and raises the woman's buttocks onto the lower part of his thigh as he penetrates her. She crosses her ankles behind his back. This reduces the depth of penetration considerably but can be very exciting for the woman who enjoys having her vaginal opening teased and stimulated.

• The man kneels between her open thighs, penetrates her, and then lifts her bottom from the bed so as to bring her as close as possible to his pelvis. This can produce superb sensations for both partners, but it is

▶ *If the woman lies close to the edge of the bed, the man can lean forward and enter her, taking most of his weight on his forearms.*

▶ *Positions that enable deep penetration are ideal for couples who want a baby (inset).*

▶ *It only takes slight variations on the man-on-top theme to produce exciting and exquisite sensations (below right).*

▼ *The woman who wants to open herself up completely to her lover, can take him into her while her legs are over his shoulders.*

tiring for the woman to keep her back arched in this way for very long. One answer is to put a couple of pillows under her bottom.

• The woman lies over the edge of the bed or a low stool with her legs open. The man enters her and leans forwards on her body, taking most of his weight on his forearms or hands. This can be very tiring for the man because movement is restricted. It is, therefore, not a very suitable position for the couple who enjoy, or need, deep thrusting during lovemaking.

• The woman lies on her side and raises her upper leg. The man cuddles into the front of her body and penetrates her. She curls her upper leg over his body. Here again, the angle of entry of the penis can be to one side, stimulating unfamiliar parts of the woman's pelvic organs. Most couples find this a very loving and restful position, as the man does not have to support his weight. However, movement is restricted and the woman may have to contract her pelvic muscles to give her man the best pleasure.

• A variation is for the woman to raise her upper leg so as to open up her pelvis

*For me nothing beats making love the old-fashioned way – with my man on top, making it all happen. Being face to face means we can kiss and cuddle while making love.*

further and 'release' him from the clamping effect around his waist. This allows him considerable movement, even though they are both on their sides, and she can obtain new sensations as she angles her upper leg differently. ❤

# REAR-ENTRY LOVEMAKING

*Of all the rear-entry positions, the 'doggy' position is almost certainly the best known. But with imagination, the loving couple can find others that are even more stimulating.*

Intercourse face to face is by far the most popular form of lovemaking, for a variety of reasons.

First, most women like to be held and have a good deal of close bodily contact during lovemaking. Second, a woman's breasts and lips – two major sources of erotic stimulation – are on the front of her body where they can be seen and 'made use of' by her lover during sex. And third, many women associate rear-entry positions with animal behavior and therefore find it a turn-off.

### MAKING THE CHANGE

For a couple who make love several times a week, however, making love in positions that involve the man penetrating the the woman from the rear can be a refreshing change and can add a touch of variety to their sex lives.

### THE G SPOT

With such a spate of recent interest in the G spot, it has been suggested by researchers that rear-entry lovemaking could actually be preferable from the woman's point of view.

In this position, the man's penis stimulates the front vaginal wall and is therefore highly exciting to a woman who has a sensitive G spot.

### PRACTICAL ADVANTAGES

Whatever the physical and emotional advantages and disadvantages of rear-entry positions, there are many prac-

tical advantages for the couple who enjoy making love in this way.

In a rear-entry position, the woman feels exceptionally vulnerable. Some women find this highly stimulating: the thought of being penetrated and taken in an 'animal-like' way greatly turns them on. However, other women find it a turn-off because they consider it an 'unromantic' position.

For all its pleasures and advantages,

▼ *For some women, rear-entry lovemaking positions that stimulate the G spot are the best way to orgasm.*

*▶ This is an ideal variation of the traditional 'doggy' position. The woman kneels on the floor, and the man, also kneeling, enters her from behind as she leans over the bed.*

rear-entry lovemaking is not very romantic. However, for many couples this is no drawback, as the woman will want to be taken with ardor on some occasions, while on others, she will want tender loving and romantic intercourse.

As human beings, we have a vast range of possibilities and this is to our advantage. It is fashionable today for women to talk about caring men in bed who spend ages with detailed and prolonged foreplay, but this should not become a boring routine, however pleasant it might be.

Many women, in therapy, say that they greatly enjoy being taken roughly. This proves to them that they are so desirable that their man cannot keep his hands off them, which is in itself sexually flattering. It also absolves them from having to put up with much foreplay which they may find contrived, boring or repetitive.

For the man who like to see his woman's bottom and anus, rear-entry positions can be extremely stimulating. If both partners like it, the man can caress her bottom, stimulate her anus and so on. Because in many rear-entry positions, the woman's thighs are at an angle to her body (this is especially true of the classical 'doggy' position) penetration is quite deep and can on occasion be very deep.

For the woman who has a sensitive G spot, rear-entry positions can be especially good. The man's penis can be arranged to hit the right spot or to massage it gently, whichever the woman prefers. Even if the woman is not sensitive to G-spot stimulation, she will experience very different sensations, many of which are highly arousing, if only because of the position's novelty to her.

A woman who is shy, who wants to fantasize about another man, or who wants to be sexually satisfied but would rather not be reminded too blatantly of her partner for some reason, may find rear entry a good way round her problem. By facing away from the man she can enjoy her partner's penis and caresses in a somewhat anonymous way.

Rear-entry positions leave the man's hands free to caress and stimulate the woman's body. In some rear-entry positions, especially the 'doggy' position, the man has more freedom to thrust and alter the amount and angle of movements his penis makes.

Rear-entry positions are ideal when a woman is pregnant and finds the missionary position too uncomfortable. But her partner must limit the depth of penetration in the last few weeks of pregnancy.

# VARIATIONS

Rear-entry positions range from the simple 'doggy' position to some highly adventurous positions that will please more athletic lovers.

Whatever variation you choose to try, make sure it suits both of you. If one partner finds a particular

position awkward, painful or tiring, this will obviously detract a great deal from his or her enjoyment.

● Probably the best-known and widely used is the 'doggy' position. The woman kneels on the bed or the floor and her partner kneels behind her and enters her. She can angle her pelvis in several different ways according to how far she leans forward and how she supports herself.

Each position gives new sensations to

▲ ▶ *If the woman lies on her front, her lover can position himself between her open legs. If he then supports his weight on his arms, he will have the flexibility of movement to thrust forcefully – if that is what she enjoys. This rear-entry position (top right) allows for relaxed, unhurried lovemaking.*

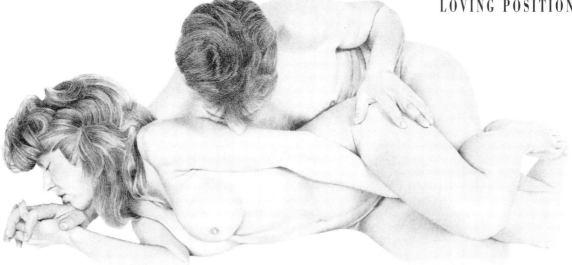

both. The woman can, for example, keep her body horizontal by resting on her hands and knees. She can rest on her elbows, or even lie with her arms back along her body, or put them under her forehead as her breasts support her upper body.

Penetration is extremely good, especially if the woman lies with her chest on the bed. The man has a large range of possible movements and the woman can be taken very forcefully, which many enjoy. A few women find that air becomes pushed into the vagina in some of these positions. This need not necessarily be a problem, but if the penis traps air and pushes it up into the top of the vagina

*Although I like rear-entry sex, I'm always anxious in case my husband decides to penetrate me anally, which I don't like. I feel very vulnerable in these positions. What should I do?*

*First, you'll have to discuss the matter with your husband and make it very plain that anal penetration isn't on.*

*He can't 'sneak up' on you and do something against your will just because you are highly aroused with rear-entry sex. For many men whose partners won't indulge in anal sex, rear-entry positions are a good compromise. The sensations are not the same, but the man who finds his partner's bottom and anus a turn-on will get much of the pleasure he would have experienced from anal intercourse.*

*Perhaps you could offer him a compromise. Say that you don't want to be penetrated anally and won't be, but that he can caress your bottom and anus when he makes love to you from behind, perhaps while he fantasizes about anal intercourse with you. This can be a practical way around a problem that could otherwise be blown up into a full-scale battle.*

◀ *Rear-entry lovemaking is exciting for many women as it allows them to feel totally vulnerable and exceptionally 'wanton'.*

▲ *Rear-entry positions are a favorite with many women as her partner can caress her body and breasts during lovemaking.*

it can cause pain. When the woman turns over the air comes out with an embarrassing noise, but most couples either ignore this or are able to make a joke out of it.

• A modification of the 'doggy' position is for the woman to kneel on a low stool or table (covered with something that cushions her knees). The man stands behind her between her open legs and enters her.

• For the more athletic, another good rear-entry position is to ask the woman to bend over with her legs wide apart and rest her hands on the floor in front of her. Her bottom and vulva are now exposed and the man can enter her.

Movement and penetration are good (at least for the man) but the woman's movements are somewhat restricted, apart from being able to wiggle her hips from side to side to enhance the pleasure. She can, as in all rear-entry positions, contract her pelvic muscles to make it more stimulating for them both.

• A restful and very enjoyable rear-entry position is 'the spoons'. The woman lies facing away from her man with her knees drawn up. The man cuddles into her body from behind and curls around and enters her. They can lie still with his penis inside her or he can move around. Penetration can be deep if she angles her body down towards the foot of the bed. He can reach round and caress the front of her body and kiss her neck and back.

• The man lies on the bed with his knees together and the woman kneels over his hips facing away from him. She takes her weight on her hands placed either side of his legs. She controls the amount of movement in this rear-entry, woman-on-top position. This position is particularly enjoyable for the bottom-centerd man as he can see her

*I ADORE FOR MY BOYFRIEND TO PENETRATE ME FROM BEHIND. IT MAKES ME FEEL VERY 'WANTON' AND BECAUSE I HAVE A VERY SENSITIVE G SPOT, I HAVE DELICIOUSLY INTENSE ORGASMS.*

bottom and anus and caress them, while his lover takes the lead.

• Another position is suitable for a woman with strong arms. Here, the woman leans over the bed, supporting her entire weight on her arms, and the man lifts her open legs off the ground and stands between them as he enters her from behind. Although movement is fairly limited in this position, penetration can be quite deep. ❤

◀ *Rear-entry positions allow deep penetration which should be both satisfying for the woman and stimulating for the man – particularly a bottom-centerd man.*

# $\mathscr{S}$IDE-BY-SIDE POSITIONS

*For couples who prize intimacy and close contact when they make love, side-by-side positions give maximum opportunity for cuddling, caressing and kissing.*

▼ *Side-entry positions allow you to get close to your partner, both physically and emotionally.*

Most couples like to bring variety into their sex lives by using positions that suit their mood at the time. And for couples who make love several times a week, lovemaking can range from the warm and intimate to the highly adventurous.

Athletic positions which require the couple to be fit and supple can be highly enjoyable from time to time, but they do have their drawbacks.

Many of the more adventurous positions, while providing stimulation in new and different ways, are often tiring and are rarely romantic.

## POSITIONS FOR INTIMACY

Side-entry positions allow for maximum body contact, are restful, and are ideal for occasions when intimacy is the order of the day. They are particularly useful when one or both partners are tired, or when the woman is pregnant.

In many of the side-entry positions the man is able to cuddle his partner, and his hands are free to caress her. And for the couple who like their lovemaking to be accompanied by words of love, these are among the best positions for intimate conversation.

### 'SPOONS' POSITION

The best known of these positions is known as the 'spoons'. This is an exceptionally good position to use during pregnancy because the woman's stomach can lie flat on the bed and it is very restful for her in the

*▲ This position is ideal for the man who likes to watch his partner's vulval area when making love. Penetration is good and both partners can reach the woman's clitoris to stimulate it. The man can also caress her all over.*

*I have difficulty getting an erection when I am tired and can only do so if I kiss my fiancée for a long time very deeply. Would a side-entry lovemaking position be good for this?*

*Yes it would. Experiment with one of the face-to-face ones – especially the one in which she draws her legs up and you lie between them as she encircles your body with them. Because you are lying down side by side it is very restful and because there is so much skin contact it is very loving. This position should give you all the stimulation you need, but you could get your fiancée to add to it by contracting her pelvic muscles and gripping your penis as you thrust.*

> *Now that I am heavily pregnant my husband and I are finding it more and more difficult to make love in comfort. But we have discovered that the 'spoons' position is ideal because I hardly have to move while he stimulates me!*

It is a very pleasant position for the couple who like to fall asleep after sex – in fact it is quite possible to go to sleep with the penis still in the vagina.

## VARIATIONS

A variation on this position is for the woman, once penetrated, to roll over on to her back a little and to place one leg over the upper leg of the man. This opens up her vulva considerably and leaves her clitoris available for her or her partner to caress. She now has both hands free to caress herself, or her lover.

Her stomach is totally free, again making this position good for late on in pregnancy. Penetration can be good but not exceptionally deep, and any thrusting movement is somewhat restricted.

From the woman's point of view it is restful and she can stimulate herself and her partner's scrotum. In some women the man's penis stimulates the G spot in this position, giving extra sensations.

The couple lie on their sides facing one another. The woman draws up her legs to her chest and opens them widely. The man then enters her while

last few months of pregnancy.

The couple lie on their sides with the man cuddling into the woman's back as she draws her knees up towards her stomach. He then tucks into her and penetrates her.

Penetration can be very good, especially if the woman angles her body down towards her feet and the man can, in a limited way, make thrusting movements. He can reach around and stimulate her clitoris or she can open her legs and do so herself. He can also reach round and caress her breasts and stomach and, at the same time, kiss her neck and back. The area of skin contact is extensive and this can be very romantic and sensuous.

▼ *A variation of the 'spoons' position, where the woman places one leg over her partner's thigh, is ideal for the female who enjoys a good deal of clitoral stimulation.*

*I have very small breasts that
have unpleasant stretch marks
since my last baby. Is there any
good position in which my
husband won't see my breasts yet
could still caress them?*

*Yes. Side-entry positions from
behind, such as the 'spoons', are
very good. Your husband can
reach around and play with your
breasts and nipples but can't see
them unless he makes a
considerable effort.*

*Having said this, you are
probably making a fuss about
nothing because your breasts are
probably not as awful as you
make out. Most men say that they
are delighted with their partner's
body even if it has stretch marks,
scars or whatever. In therapy
many such men say 'what stretch
marks?' They simply aren't aware
of them yet their women are very
upset by them. Try to remember
that your partner loves you for
what you are – stretch marks,
small breasts or any other
imperfections.*

▲ *The 'spoons' position
is one of the most
comfortable and
affectionate of the
positions because the
man can easily kiss and
talk intimately to her.*

▼ *Here, the position of
the woman's legs does
restrict her partner's
thrusting movements
during penetration, but
he is able to caress her
body and easily kiss her
breasts if this is what
she likes.*

the woman folds her legs around his
back. She also cuddles him around the
shoulders with her arms.

Penetration can be very good but
movement is somewhat restricted. The
couple can kiss very easily and passionately. There is a lot of skin contact and
this can make the couple feel very
much 'at one' with each other.

This position is not suitable for very
overweight people or for women who
are pregnant.

### SIDE-ENTRY POSITION
One of the best lovemaking positions of
all is a side-entry one. The woman lies
on her back and the man on his side at
right angles to her body. The woman
can then draw her thighs back towards
her stomach while he enters her as he
lies underneath her.

Penetration is deep and movement
can be good, but not excellent.
It is another restful position
during pregnancy or for the
larger woman. Both part-
ners can reach the
woman's clitoris to stimulate it and the man can
caress most parts of her
body, including her
breasts. The only real

*MY GIRLFRIEND AND I HAVE TRIED A VARIETY OF POSITIONS DURING LOVEMAKING – SOME CONVENTIONAL AND SOME RATHER ADVENTUROUS. BUT FOR SHEER LUXURIOUS AND INTIMATE PLEASURE, LYING SIDE BY SIDE WHILE MAKING LOVE IS HARD TO BEAT. WE CAN TAKE OUR TIME AND CARESS AND CUDDLE EACH OTHER AT A SLOWER PACE.*

▼ *Movement is easier here and penetration can be quite deep, particularly if the woman raises her bottom off the bed a little. The woman cannot play a very active role, but her partner can caress her breasts and kiss her shoulders.*

disadvantage is that they cannot kiss.

It is a good position for a 'quickie' because it involves very little undressing. It is also good for conceiving, especially if the woman remains with her legs in the drawn-back position for a few minutes after intercourse. The woman can also reach the man's scrotum.

The anus of both partners is accessible for those who like anal stimulation

and it is a good position for inexperienced women who have difficulty having orgasms during intercourse.

### LEVELS OF PENETRATION

The woman lies on her side, turning slightly on to her front and supporting her top half with her forearms on the bed. The man cuddles into her back just as in the spoons positions, then puts his upper leg over her hips as he penetrates her.

It is a pleasant position for the man to be able to caress the woman's back with one hand but she can do very little. Penetration is not especially good because her legs are fairly straight, but he is allowed quite good movement.

By drawing her knees up to her stomach she can increase penetration, but the position then converts into the more restful and satisfactory 'spoons'.

This position is also ideal for a woman who is making love for the first time after she has given birth. It is a time when a woman may be wary of

▼ *The woman places her leg over her man's upper leg for deep penetration. Movement is limited but both partners can kiss.*

deep penetration, especially if she has had an episiotomy. Also, she may have tender breasts if she is breastfeeding.

She can start off making love with her legs fairly straight, thus limiting penetration, and, as her confidence grows, she can draw her knees up. But at all times she will be in control and this can ease any fears she may have. ❤

*I need a great deal of clitoral stimulation if I am to come during intercourse. Really I like a vibrator playing on me all the time. Is there a good position in which this can be done?*

*Yes – the side-entry position in which the man lies at right angles under your thighs. You can stimulate your clitoris with the vibrator and your man can penetrate you and stroke you all over.*

▲ *The woman lies on her front, her bottom slightly raised, and the man lies over her at right angles and penetrates her from behind.*

71

# ⒶDVANCED LOVEMAKING

*For the loving couple who want to experiment occasionally,
there is always the opportunity to try something new.*

Ⓜaking love does not differ much between East and West. It is just that the East has all the good books. The Indian *Kama Sutra*, the Arabian *Perfumed Garden* and the Chinese and Japanese pillow books have all helped to systematize sexual behavior and to allow people to try what others have tried before – and found successful and enjoyed – without just relying on their intuition.

### THE FRENCH WAY

The French have put a lot of thought into lovemaking; and they have come up with all sorts of interesting names for the more advanced sexual positions.

• The *flanquette* positions – in the flanquette, or 'man-on-top', positions the man lies face to face with his partner but has only one of his legs between hers.

He can either lie directly on top of her, or they can lie side by side. Or they can roll about until they discover the most comfortable of the intermediate positions for themselves.

All the *flanquette* positions allow deep penetration and the position of the man's thigh also helps to ensure good clitoral stimulation. Many men also find the woman's thigh rubbing against their testicles stimulating, although some men may find the idea threatening. Be careful to keep movements fluid, how-

▼ *Foreplay is an important part of lovemaking. Many men find it arousing if the woman is dominant.*

▼ *The* **flanquette** *position here is with the man lying facing his partner with one leg between hers. This position is good for deep penetration. The man can use his thigh to stimulate the clitoris.*

ever. Any sudden movement of the woman's leg could be painful.

### REAR ENTRY

The French often call rear-entry position coitus *à la négresse*. Rear-entry positions were considered bestial, and much too base for 'civilized' Europeans to use. They were thought to be only suitable for the 'inferior' heathen races. Such positions were often seen as submissive as far as the woman was concerned, and it may be that *à la négresse* has something to do with the advantage white plantation owners took of their female slaves in the past. In fact, the *à la négresse* position requires the female to be active and does not mean she has been put in a 'humiliating' position.

She starts by lying face down with her hands clasped behind her neck and with her buttocks in the air. When the man enters her,

*MY BOYFRIEND AND I LIKE THE REAR-ENTRY POSITION BEST. IF HE LIES NEXT TO ME, THREADS HIS LEG UNDER ONE OF MINE AND THEN OVER THE OTHER, HE CAN PENETRATE ME FULLY AND DEEPLY. THE POSITION ALLOWS HIM TO FACE ME BY PROPPING HIMSELF UP ON HIS ELBOW.*

she hooks her legs round his and uses them to pull him onto her. Using her legs in this way means that the apparently submissive woman can actually control the pace and depth of love-making.

### 'CUISSADE' POSITIONS

The *cuissade* positions are similar, except that the man takes the woman half from the rear. Usually the woman lies on her back and the man lies beside her, then threads his leg under one of hers and over the other, effectively turning her pelvis. From here, he can enter her from the rear, while propping himself up on his elbow so that they can still look at each other.

The *cuissade* positions allow the man's penis to enter the vagina at some very stimulating angles. Or, if he remains lying on his side, this is a very leisurely position for both partners – although none the less stimulating for that. It is one of those positions that a couple can finish an exhausting day with, as it allows them to fall asleep while their genitals are still locked together. And if approached gently, it can be an interest-

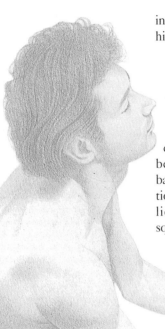

ing and sensual way for a man to wake his partner in the morning.

### THE VIENNESE OYSTER

The Austrians are also adventurous if what is termed the Viennese Oyster position is to be believed.

This can only be performed by an extremely supple woman. She must be able to cross her feet behind the back of her head. She assumes this position lying on her back. The man then lies full length on top of her and squeezes her feet. Apart from the stimulation of the soles of the

feet, this position allows a unique rocking pelvic movement.

Those not so supple should try bringing their knees up to their shoulders and crossing their ankles on their stomach. Either way, the woman must be able to get into this position voluntarily.

### SEX FLORENTINE

Coitus *à la Florentine* allows a woman to enjoy a man even though he is not fully erect. She simply holds back his penile skin – and his foreskin if he is uncircumcised – with her forefinger and thumb so that it is stretched tight – both when it is going in and when it is coming out. This sometimes makes the penis firm enough for intercourse, even if the man is not aroused at all.

The woman can also use the same technique to control – usually to speed up – the time he takes to ejaculate.

For the average awake, sober and potent man Florentine sex is extremely stimulating.

Once a couple has progressed past the missionary position, the woman-on-top positions provide excellent variations. This is all to the good. They increase penetration, aid clitoral stimulation and allow the woman to take control so that she can hold back the man's

▲ *The Viennese Oyster needs a supple woman. The woman lies back and rests her knees on her shoulders. The man squeezes her feet as he enters her.*

▼ *This woman-on-top position allows full contact along both partners' bodies. The woman rests the soles of her feet on the man's.*

*WE'VE STARTED GOING TO YOGA CLASSES SO THAT WE CAN BECOME MORE SUPPLE AND EXTEND OUR LOVEMAKING REPERTOIRE. IT'S HELPED A LOT AFTER ONLY A FEW SESSIONS – AND WE HAVE FUN TRYING OUT INDIVIDUAL EXERCISES TOO!*

ejaculation until she is fulfilled enough and ready to have her own orgasm.

## THE WANTON WOMAN

Few men can resist the woman who takes the initiative in sex. A new dimension can be added to the simplest woman-on-top position if the woman rests the soles of her feet on the top of the man's feet. This will make the woman splay her legs, and gives the name to the position – the frog.

Here, the man and the woman have direct and complete contact all the way down the front of their legs.

## SUPERIOR VARIATION

Once the straightforward woman-on-top positions have been mastered, it is possible to become more adventurous.

From the straight kneeling-on-top position, the woman can manoeuvre one leg so that it is under the man's thigh, then bring her other leg over that same side and rest it on his shoulder.

Now, still sitting on him, she can lean back so that his penis applies the maximum pressure on the front of her vagina. This is known as the X position and prolongs intercourse.

It is often difficult for the woman to balance in this posi-

◀ *The X position requires the couple to face each other and the woman positions her legs – one on the man's shoulder, the other between his legs – to form what looks like the letter X.*

75

> *MY MAN AND I PREFER THE WOMAN-ON-TOP POSITION BECAUSE IT GIVES HIM A CHANCE TO USE LESS ENERGY WHILE I STIMULATE HIM. I LIKE IT BECAUSE I HAVE MORE CONTROL.*

tion and she may need to hold her lover around the neck or grasp his hand.

### STAGECOACH

The best of all female superior sexual positions is what the French call 'the stagecoach to Lyon'. In this position, the man lies on his back and the woman kneels astride him, facing away. Once his penis is fully inserted, she leans back and rests her weight on her hands. Then she moves her legs around so that her feet are resting flat either side of him.

Not only does this put pressure on her G spot, it stimulates his penis and gives him an arousing view of her body.

In this position, she can bounce up and down like the proverbial 'stage-coach to Lyon'. But that is not the end of it. From here, the woman can move around, first so that her body lies across his. Then she can

▲▼ *In the wheelbarrow and stagecoach (below) positions, the woman can support herself while her partner enters her from behind.*

▶ *Making love standing up can put stress on the woman unless she is supported. Hold onto each other's buttocks for extra support.*

turn right around so that her body faces his, but her weight is supported on her hands and feet alone.

### FURNITURE FUN

The simplest woman-on-top position – out of bed – is on a chair. If the man sits down, the woman can simply sit astride him, face to face. Many wooden dining chairs have low rungs at the front, where the man can rest his feet, and higher ones at the side, for hers.

But then she can also sit on his lap, facing away from him. Chairs, like most furniture, can be an endless source of erotic amusement. Try making love over the back of the chair.

### STANDING UP

Many young couples make love standing up in public places, often because they do not have anywhere else to go. The classic 'knee-trembler' can be an unpleasant strain unless the woman is a little taller than the man. If not, telephone books are useful props, as they allow you to adjust the height until it is just right. The bottom step of the stairs is usually the right height as well. But be careful. Often during orgasm your legs can go very weak and this could lead to an unfortunate accident. It is really safest to do it against a wall or some other solid object that can be used for support. With free-standing

▶ *This position is only for the very strong and very supple. The man supports the woman by holding her waist as she hangs upside-down.*

sex, remember to bend your knees and support each other.

### TAKING IT FURTHER

Once you have mastered the techniques involved in making love standing, you can move on. If her partner is strong enough – and has a well-developed sense of balance – a woman can first curl one leg up around his buttocks, as in advanced Indian love positions, then lock both her legs around his waist, supporting the rest of her weight by locking her arms around his neck.

If both partners are athletic enough, she can release her grip on his neck and fall back until she is upside-down.

Remember, advanced lovemaking should not be an end in itself. An occasional journey into unexplored territory is usually enough to add excitement into a couple's sex life. ❤

*I like to think of myself as fairly adventurous in bed, but some of the advanced positions seem rather dangerous. What is the dividing line between athletic sex and contortionist positions?*

*Some of the really athletic positions – like those listed in the Kama Sutra – should only be explored by extremely fit and supple lovers. The golden rule for the rest of us is to go with what feels comfortable. If there is the slightest hint of trouble, stop.*

# POSITIONS FOR ADVANCED LOVING

*Cosy, erotic, athletic and bizarre – all of these words can be used to describe the wide variety of positions available to imaginative lovers.*

In most relationships, a couple will try out a number of positions for lovemaking early on, and then settle for the three or four that they find suit them best. There is nothing wrong with this – if the couple is happy with them, they are well served by what they like best. Yet, lovemaking takes place under so many varying conditions, and in so many moods, that you should explore all the options.

### HOW MANY POSITIONS?

'Experts' have differed over the centuries as to how many positions a couple might use to make love. One researcher reckoned that there were as many as 10,000 ranging from the run-of-the-mill missionary position to the unorthodox, athletic and bizarre. In reality, there are five basic positions for lovemaking: man on top (known as the missionary position), woman on top, rear entry, side entry and standing.

The missionary position is probably the most

▼ *A woman-on-top position gives the man deep, satisfying penetration.*

popular of all positions for lovemaking. It allows the man to take the lead, and it is romantic in that the couple can see each other at all times. Most couples return to the missionary position again and again after trying others.

Woman-on-top positions have a number of advantages as well. In all the variations it is the woman who takes control. Also, her hands are free to caress her partner or to help bring herself to orgasm. She can either face him as they make love, or she can face away from him.

Rear-entry or 'doggie-style' lovemaking is for more urgent, aggressive lovemaking. The man is free to thrust more powerfully than in any other position and some lovers find that this brings an animal-like quality to their lovemaking, which they may welcome from time to time. The woman can respond as much or as little as she likes. Its only disadvantage is that the woman cannot see what her partner is doing.

Side entry is relaxing and satisfying with the man taking the woman from the side rather than the rear.

It is relaxing

> *FOR A REALLY MEMORABLE LOVEMAKING SESSION, MY PARTNER AND I LIKE TO CHANGE POSITIONS SEVERAL TIMES AS WE MAKE LOVE. THIS MEANS THAT WE CAN TAKE TURNS SEIZING THE INITIATIVE AND CONTROLLING THE PACE.*

▲ *The position known as Banks of the Nile is one that gives the woman unparalleled scope for movement. The man lies on his back on the bed and brings his knees back towards his chest, allowing the woman to sit half-way up his thighs. Once his penis is in her vagina, she can bounce up and down, swivel and use both her hands to massage her clitoris and bring herself to simultaneous orgasm with her lover.*

because it can only be performed lying down and, because the man wraps his body around the woman, body contact is at a maximum.

Standing positions are probably best left for the times when a couple fancy a quickie or they are feeling more athletic than usual, although there is no doubt, given that the time, the setting and the mood are right, that these positions have a rare charm all their own.

### WHEN TO USE THEM

Often the key to a memorable bout of lovemaking is not to start off in a favorite position but to change positions as you make love. This style of love-making lends itself particularly to the couple who know each other's pet likes and dislikes. If the man has good penile control and can sense when the tempo needs to be increased, or the mood soft-ened, the positions can be changed not just once, but several times. Equally, the woman may suddenly wish to change

from a passive to a more active role. What started off as a slow, romantic session may well become more frenzied as passion takes over.

### VARY THE PLACE

Of course, the wise lover recognizes that it is not just a good position that makes for advanced lovemaking. A new place or a different time of day can turn even an old favorite into something new and memorable. And for those who really do not want to make a major change from what they like best, they can always try a subtle switch of position during the course of their lovemaking.

The sensations of both partners in a man-on-top position, for example, can become quite novel if the woman raises her legs and clasps them around her partner's waist, or places them over his shoulders. A rear-entry position where the woman is lying face downwards on the bed can change dramatically if she raises her buttocks and offers them up to her partner.

And both positions can become com-pletely different if they are tried out on the floor, or perhaps in the open air – weather and decency permitting.

### BACK TO BASICS

Some variations of the basic positions are so minute that they barely differ from the originals. But others are worth

> *My girlfriend and I have tried all sorts of positions for lovemaking and we like nearly all of them. Yet, while some of them seem to give her a lot of pleasure, others are better for me. Why?*
>
> *Obviously the easiest way for a man to put his penis into a woman's vagina is straight in so that the length of the penis is parallel with the vaginal walls. Yet, because of the variations of sensations that a woman is capable of, it obviously makes sense to vary the angle of approach. If, say, the woman has a sensitive G spot, it makes sense to choose a position where the G spot, situated on the front wall of the vagina, is stimulated. It is also important to bear in mind that the only part of the actual vagina that is sensitive is its opening. The depths of the vagina are, for most women, unable to sense anything other than movement. Perhaps this is why so many women say that the size of their man's penis does not matter to them. Accept the situation and enjoy the positions that give both of you pleasure.*

trying for the differing sensations they provide for one – or both – partners.

### MAN ON TOP

The basic man-on-top position has both partners lying down, the man entering the woman with his legs between hers, her legs drawn up and her feet resting on the bed. There are several interesting alternatives.

The woman can straighten her legs and keep them spread wide on the bed rather than raising them. The man enters her in the same way but, because her vulva is now pointing straight ahead rather than upwards and towards her partner, the angle is subtly different. The man's penis is naturally pointing upwards and he is therefore able to stimulate her G spot to greater effect. The sensations for him will be slightly different as well.

The man can lie with his legs outside the woman's. Now, he can use his thighs to squeeze hers together, and her thighs will, in turn, compress his penis. If the woman expands and contracts her pelvic

▶ *When the woman is astride her lover and facing him, she can bring her body down on his, and skim his chest with her breasts, while he uses his hands to push her ever closer to him to reach deeper and deeper inside her.*

muscles while they are making love, she can provide markedly different sensations for the man. This variation is recommended for women after childbirth.

If a pillow or two can be placed under the woman's bottom, sensations in any of the man-on-top positions will become different as penetration will be deeper. The angle of the man's penis will be slightly different as well.

### WOMAN ON TOP

The basic woman-on-top position is used by the majority of couples when the woman wants to take control of their lovemaking. She sits with her back erect, her knees resting on the bed by the side of the man.

She can place the soles of her feet on the upper surfaces of her partner's feet and both of them can spread their legs wide apart with their knees bent.

The position with the woman on top facing away is almost as widely used as the basic position, but novel and exciting sensations can be achieved during intercourse for both partners if the woman turns right round very slowly from one position to the other.

The woman can squat over the man's penis but if,

instead of kneeling, she straightens her legs and rests them on his shoulders, she can then move up and down at her own pace. Of all the woman-on-top positions, this is the one that allows the woman to turn right round with little risk of injury to the man. It also enables the man's penis to stimulate her at every possible angle. All he is required to do is maintain his erection and control the time that he climaxes.

### REAR ENTRY

The most popular of all rear-entry positions is where the woman lies face down on the bed, with her buttocks raised. The man kneels and enters her. Either of the partners can direct his penis into her vagina. Here are just a handful of the satisfying variations to the basic position.

▼ *The Wild Geese position is ideal for the woman who enjoys having her clitoris stimulated. It should not be attempted if the woman is pregnant.*

If the woman lies flat on her face on the bed with her legs as wide apart as is comfortable for her, entry may be a little more complicated but the position provides the man with a different angle. It is also more restful for the woman, although it does restrict her movement.

Instead of kneeling between the woman's legs, the man can place his knees on either side of her so that he can ease forward until he is virtually sitting astride her back. The sensation is closer to 'riding' the woman than any other of the rear-entry positions. Lovemaking in this position should not be hurried and is unlikely to succeed if the woman has not been stimulated earlier with some creative foreplay.

For the fit and athletic, there are endless variations to basic positions. Here are four of them.

### THE RUTTING DEER

This is a variation of the man-on-top position that allows deep penetration and determined thrusting from the man.

himself on his hands, thrusting forwards.

To make penetration even deeper, the woman can bring her knees further back and rest them on her partner's shoulders. Lose-limbed, athletic women may even be able to cross their legs behind his neck.

### PARTING OF THE WAVES

Although movement by both partners is limited, this position allows a unique angle of penetration.

The main problem lies in taking up the position. To do this, the woman should lie back near the edge of the bed and raise her legs in the air. The man kneels by her side facing towards her feet and should then be able to enter her. Then, as he slowly leans forward, the woman lies back. The man takes his weight on his hands on the floor while the woman uses her hands on his buttocks to assist his thrusting.

### REACH FOR THE SKY

Although this is not one of the most romantic positions, it nevertheless offers a unique angle of penetration for the man and therefore very different sensations for the woman. The woman lies on her back as comfortably as she can and parts her legs, raising them skywards. To start off with, the man should kneel over her thighs while facing towards her feet. Then, as she raises her legs, he can enter her. The angle of his penis means that he will be hitting the back wall of her vagina so this is no good for G-spot stimulation. However, he is free to thrust as hard as they both

The top part of the woman's body need not move but she can contribute to their lovemaking by determined pelvic movement with the lower half of her body – both up and down and rotating from side to side.

The woman lies back on the bed, the upper half of her body on the bed and her legs resting on the floor. Ideally, her buttocks should be resting on the bed. The man approaches her and, as he enters her, she bends her knees back towards her stomach while he supports

▲ *Most couples find that after they experiment with some of the more unusual positions, they come back to the missionary position time and time again.*

▼ *Reach for the Sky allows the man to move sideways but is no good for G-spot stimulation.*

enjoy and the position also allows for considerable sideways movement from the man.

For the couple who enjoy fantasizing as they make love, this position offers unique possibilities as, unless the man contorts his neck to look behind, neither partner can see the other.

### WILD GEESE

The strength of this position is that it allows unique access for the man to use his hands on the woman's clitoris to control the pace of her orgasm. It is also more comfortable than it looks for the woman. It should only be attempted if there is a long rug or thick carpet on the floor next to the bed.

The woman rests her buttocks on the bed and straightens her back on the floor until she is comfortable. She can use the man's feet to support her head if need be. The man then sits on the bed between her legs and draws her towards him.

Because potential for pelvic movement from both partners is limited, this is a particularly suitable position if the man feels that he is in

*▼ Most women like to be stimulated with imaginative foreplay to maximize the satisfaction they get from rear-entry lovemaking which should never be rushed.*

*My husband says that he likes positions where he gets the deepest penetration. Which are the best positions for this?*

*Most, if not all, men like deep penetration, especially at the moment that they have their orgasm. The deepest penetration is possible in positions where the woman's thighs are pressed back towards her body. Also, positions such as those where the woman lies on her back with her knees up to her breasts, or she is on all fours, allow the man's penis to be inserted deeply into her vagina. The more her thighs are in line with her body and the more they are closed, the less the penetration. If you do not like penetration to be too deep, you can control it by using one of the woman-on-top positions.*

danger of coming too quickly, which can often happen when taking up one of the more adventurous lovemaking positions. The woman can hold his penis inside her, contracting her pelvic muscles to grip him. If the couple wish to increase the pace, it is then a simple matter for the man to draw the woman up so that she is squatting over him. The initiative can then come from the woman.   ❤

# 3

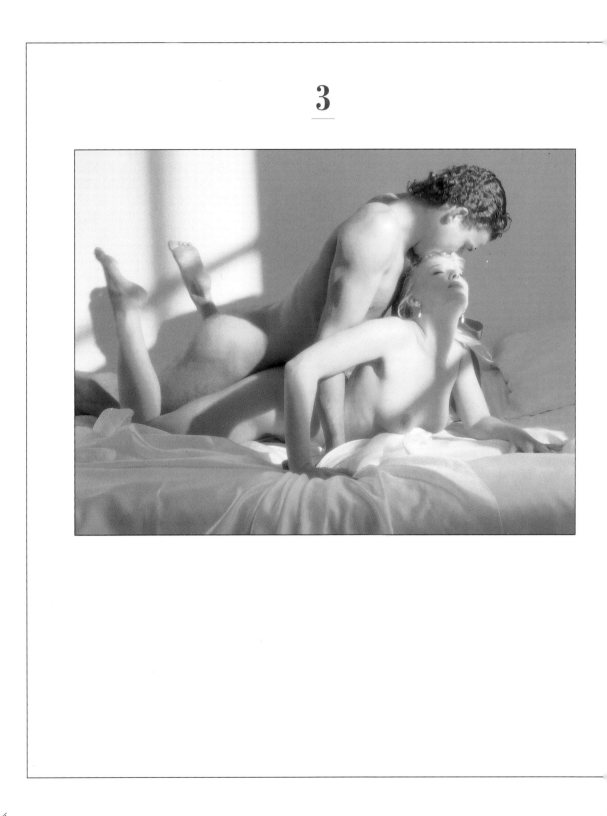

# Perfect Orgasms

Having an orgasm is the climax of making love, and caring lovers take trouble to ensure that both partners achieve this when possible. Because it is a biological necessity that they should ejaculate, men often reach orgasm easily, but some women can find it more difficult. These pages contain advice for such women and their lovers. Simultaneous orgasm is a special delight, but not something to try for every time you make love. Aim simply to enjoy yourselves.

# $\mathcal{S}$IMULTANEOUS ORGASM

*For the loving couple, being attuned to each other so that they come at exactly the same time can be the ultimate goal of their lovemaking. The secret is balancing their sexual pace.*

◀ *Attaining a simultaneous orgasm usually means speeding up the woman's response as well as slowing down the man. This position leaves the man with both hands free – one can caress her clitoris while the other stimulates her body elsewhere.*

$\mathcal{F}$or many couples, the 'ideal' form of lovemaking is one in which they both have an orgasm at the same time – anything else is considered to be poor by comparison. Certainly, when orgasms do come together in this way they can be very pleasant, but to make love with this goal always in mind is to store up a measure of disappointment and resentment for the future.

### TRYING TOO HARD

Try to imagine lovemaking as a dinner party where the purpose is to enjoy the food and the company of the guests. If you were to commit yourself to swallowing the last morsel of food at exactly the same time as your partner you would be preoccupied with timing, would not concentrate on the meal and, as a result, would not enjoy it. And then suppose you did both finish the last piece of food at exactly the same time – would the occasion be any the better?

Unfortunately, for many couples the whole business of simultaneous orgasms is much the same – the very act of trying to come together prevents it from happening. The stress involved in trying to hold off his own orgasm can be very tiring for a man. It can interfere with his ejaculatory timing and so reduce the pleasure he gets from his orgasm. For the woman, things can be stressful if she hurries her own orgasm to coincide with his.

### ORGASM IN INTERCOURSE

For men, an orgasm is an essential part of the procreative act. Without it, he cannot impregnate a woman. Male orgasm is thus a biological necessity.

But female orgasm is much more elusive and less clear cut. All that is necessary, biologically, is that the woman is sufficiently receptive so that the man can place his semen near her cervix. Orgasm during intercourse is not necessary.

Of those women who do have orgasms, twice as many get them from manual or oral clitoral stimulation as from intercourse. A

▶ *While simultaneous orgasms are certainly very pleasant, they should not be regarded as the be-all and end-all of sexual intercourse. Making love should be a pleasure for both partners and not a chore or a difficult exercise for either.*

US survey of 106,000 women in 1980 found that 34 per cent usually had orgasms from intercourse. So if simultaneous orgasms are to occur during intercourse – which is what most people mean when they use the phrase – few people are likely to experience them.

Orgasms are found to be less common among younger and unmarried women than in older women. A national women's magazine survey in the UK in 1984 found that 42 per cent of wives reached orgasm through

" *MY BOYFRIEND AND I HAVE A VERY ENJOYABLE SEX LIFE. BUT THE MOST TOTALLY SATISFYING TIMES FOR BOTH OF US ARE WHEN WE ACHIEVE SIMULTANEOUS ORGASM. HE BRINGS ME TO THE POINT OF ORGASM ORALLY, THEN I GO ON TOP AND HE STIMULATES MY CLITORIS WITH HIS HAND UNTIL WE BOTH COME TOGETHER.* "

intercourse alone, compared to 24 per cent of unmarried women. Clearly, practice and familiarity help women relax sufficiently to enjoy orgasms during intercourse.

From these findings it appears that the chance of having any orgasm – including a simultaneous one – during intercourse rises as a woman grows older – particularly if she is married.

### SOME MYTHS DISPELLED

Some men blame their women for being 'frigid' if they do not have an orgasm

▼ *When the woman is on top, she can also better stimulate the walls of her vagina.*

during intercourse and especially at the same time. This is grossly unfair as frigidity is an entirely different thing from an inability to have orgasm.

Frigidity means an inability to respond sexually, in any way. To many men, a woman who cannot, or does not, have an orgasm (and preferably during intercourse) is in some way lacking. This is an unfortunate and harmful concept because it judges women's sexuality by the same standards as men's.

Women who do not have orgasms are not neurotic – at least no more so than men who are impotent – and most women's maternal feelings place a higher value on giving pleasure than on receiving it.

### LEARNING THE SQUEEZE TECHNIQUE

THE MAN SHOULD BECOME AROUSED BY READING SOMETHING EROTIC AND PRODUCE AN ERECTION BY MASTURBATING. WHEN HE HAS A REALLY HARD ERECTION HE SHOULD STOP THE STIMULATION AND SQUEEZE THE HEAD OF HIS PENIS BETWEEN FINGERS AND THUMB AROUND THE RIM. THIS WILL MAKE THE ERECTION SUBSIDE VERY QUICKLY. ONCE HIS PENIS IS FLACCID, HE SHOULD RE-STIMULATE IT IN HIS FAVORITE WAY AND GO ON WITH THE CYCLE OF AROUSAL AND STOPPING FOR AS LONG AS HE CAN BEAR IT. HE SHOULD BUILD UP THE TIME HE CAN HOLD OFF HAVING AN ORGASM UNTIL HE CAN GO COMFORTABLY FOR HALF AN HOUR.

SOME MEN GO ON TO DO ALL THIS WITH THEIR PARTNER. THIS IS GOOD TRAINING BECAUSE THE EROTIC STATUS IS MORE REALISTIC AND CLOSER TO THE TRUE INTERCOURSE CONDITIONS. THE WOMAN WHO IS TRAINING HER MAN CAN STIMULATE HIM HOWEVER SHE THINKS BEST AND THEN SQUEEZE HIM TO MAKE HIS ERECTION GO DOWN.

AFTER A FEW DAYS OF THIS TRAINING, THE MAN SHOULD BE ABLE TO BE GIVEN AN ERECTION AND BE LEFT FOR SOME TIME WITHOUT EJACULATING. HE COULD, PERHAPS, DO A JOB AROUND THE HOUSE OR CARRY OUT A PERSONAL TASK FOR HIS PARTNER. THE COUPLE THEN BRING HIM TO ERECTION AGAIN.

AS LONG AS THE TRAINING SESSIONS ALWAYS END WITH INTERCOURSE OR MASTURBATION FOR THE MAN, NO PROBLEMS WILL RESULT.

AFTER A FEW WEEKS ALMOST ANY MAN WILL BE ABLE TO HOLD OFF HIS ORGASM AT WILL FOR ALMOST ANY LENGTH OF TIME. THE SECRET IS FOR HIM TO BECOME AWARE OF WHEN HE IS ABOUT TO REACH THE POINT OF 'NO RETURN'. HE THEN TELLS OR SIGNALS TO HIS PARTNER THAT HIS ORGASM IS IMMINENT AND SHE STOPS STIMULATING HIM. LATER IN INTERCOURSE HE CAN RECOGNIZE THESE SENSATIONS AND CAN STOP PENILE THRUSTING, ACTUALLY COME OUT OF HER VAGINA TO BE SQUEEZED OR DO SOMETHING ELSE TO CONTROL HIS PROGRESS TO ORGASM. AFTER THE EARLY STAGES OF TRAINING IT IS SENSIBLE TO PROCEED VERY CAUTIOUSLY TO VAGINAL PENETRATION – THIS IS BEST DONE WITH THE WOMAN ON TOP.

Men in our culture are goal-centered and see their having an orgasm as crucial to any sexual transaction. As a result, most expect their woman to have one too. A large United States survey of more than 4,000 men in 1977 found that the majority defined the end of inter-course as occurring when 'both had had an orgasm'. Many, if not most, women would disagree.

### TOWARD PERFECT TIMING

Obviously, with something as uniquely individual as a person's sexuality, there can be no hard and fast rules about how to produce simultaneous orgasms, but clinical experience does enable us to learn from others. For the majority of couples, the woman will have to speed up her orgasm, and the man hold back his, if simultaneous orgasm is to be any-thing other than a chance rarity. Here are some tips on how to achieve this.

### SPEEDING UP A WOMAN

• Oral sex beforehand is a great favorite. If a man brings a woman to near climax orally, and then penetrates her, she might well come almost at once. The final stimulation of penile thrust-ing is just enough to push such a woman over the edge to orgasm.

• For the woman whose main area of sexual excite-ment is her G spot, rear-entry sex, especially the doggy position, can help to ensure that she is stim-ulated where it matters most.

• Try using a

*I have no problems holding off for almost any length of time with my wife and she often has orgasms as I ejaculate. But recently I had sex with someone when I was away on business and I lost all control. Why was this?*

*This is a common story. You were thoroughly guilty about your extra-marital dalliance and, wanting to get it over with quickly, your unconscious mind drove you to ejaculate sooner than you would have liked. Many men in this situation can't sustain an erection at all, let alone control their orgasm delicately. Quite unconsciously, such situations raise fears of discovery, sexually transmitted diseases and unwanted pregnancies and all of these factors tend to counterbalance the excitement and adventure of a one-night stand.*

*The sort of ejaculatory control you have with your wife comes from a stable relationship.*

favorite fantasy. Some women can take themselves from being 'pleasantly warm' to 'boiling point' simply by using a particularly arousing fantasy.

• Foreplay is the answer to orgasms dur-ing intercourse for most women. This needs to be highly personalized to suit the individual woman.

• The couple should find a position in which the woman's clitoris can be stimulated easily and com-fortably. One of the

▼ *Any rear-entry position may speed up a woman's orgasm by stimulating her G spot.*

▼ *Many women find that they can control both their own orgasm and that of their partner if they are on top. Some positions, like this one, allow for clitoral stimulation as well.*

these maneuvres run the risk that the man may gain so much control that he can eventually end up unable to have an orgasm even when he wants to.

This is a real danger when meddling with male arousal. However, assuming that the man simply comes sooner than he would like to on some occasions and so cannot wait for his partner to come, here are some things that may work.

• Talk it over with your partner – she may well be able to help you. Perhaps she stimulates you too passionately or, during foreplay, brings you to the point of no return and then wonders why you come so quickly and she is not ready. The secret here is to balance your sexual paces.

• Use a sheath for a few weeks. This can so reduce sensitivity that it can break the cycle of too-quick arousal.

• Use a weak anesthetic cream or ointment on the tip of the penis. This reduces its sensitivity.

• Contract your anus tightly at the end of each thrust.

best positions in which to do this is for the man to lie at right angles to his partner's body and under her raised and parted thighs. This leaves both hands free so that one can caress her clitoris while the other pleasures her elsewhere on her body.

### SLOWING DOWN A MAN

This is rather more difficult than speeding up a woman and the couple who try

*My boyfriend gets me so aroused that I come very soon after he penetrates me. The problem is that he then goes on making love for hours after that and I find all the bumping and grinding rather boring once I've had my orgasm. What can I do to speed him up?*

*It may help if you concentrate more on stimulating your boyfriend and discourage him from arousing you more than is necessary for penetration. Once the initial contractions of orgasm are over, the muscles of the vaginal wall relax and as, by this time, they will be wet and very well lubricated, he may be getting very little sensation on his penis. It may help if you stop for a minute and dry your vagina, then stimulate him manually or orally before letting him penetrate you again. Try a position where he does not penetrate you so deeply. After orgasm, the top of the vagina is greatly expanded and it is likely that the sensitive head of the penis is getting very little stimulation at all.*

*You could, of course, enjoy your first orgasm, then aim for a second when your boyfriend ejaculates. Or if your boyfriend really does go on for a long time, you may be able to enjoy several orgasms before he eventually comes.*

*But this is something that you will have to work out between yourselves. Discuss it with him. He may be flattered that he can make you come over and over again. On the other hand, he may be experiencing some problem of his own that, with loving care, you can help him work out.*

▼ *If the woman has one orgasm before intercourse, this can make a penetration-induced orgasm much more likely.*

• Focus your attention on something non-sexual to distract you temporarily from too-fast arousal.

### LEARNING THE SIGNS

Ejaculation training for men enables a woman to learn in detail the warning signs of her man's imminent orgasm. This can be useful if she is try-ing to time an orgasm to coincide with his, or wants to slow him down.

A loving and caring man will learn by careful observation of his partner what her final arousal signs are so that he can let go at the same time.

### A NOTE OF CAUTION

If producing simultaneous orgasms detracts from enjoyment of sex, you should stop trying. It probably makes sense not to try for them too often and to allow yourselves to enjoy sponta-neous intercourse most of the time. ❤

# PERFECT TIMING

*Climaxing together is not essential in order to make sex enjoyable, but when it does happen, it can make lovemaking memorable – for both partners.*

Most lovers would like every lovemaking session to end in orgasm for both partners, preferably at the same time. Many couples find this difficult to achieve, yet with care and sensitivity, simultaneous orgasm is well within the scope of most loving couples.

### TIMING

Generally, a woman takes longer to reach orgasm, so she will need more creative foreplay than the man, who, left to his own devices, can usually achieve orgasm in three minutes, or less.

Ironically, many women who cannot come during conventional intercourse are perfectly able to reach orgasm through masturbation, oral sex or with a vibrator. The answer is to choose a position where the woman can stimulate her clitoris – generally the woman-on-top position – or one where the man can do it for her.

In any event, the golden rule for simultaneous orgasm lies in timing. Of course, getting the timing right is not that simple. Some women are multi-orgasmic, some only rarely have orgasms, while the quality of a man's orgasm can also vary quite surprisingly.

### WHO TAKES CHARGE?

In lovemaking sessions, it is important that one partner takes control. This can be done in a number of ways.

For example, if the man feels his own orgasm approaching without any sign of his partner's, he can either control the pace of intercourse by keeping his thrusting to a minimum while caressing his partner, or he can withdraw his penis and arouse her with his fingers, mouth or vibrator before entering her again. The lover who is in tune with his partner will know, also,

▼ *Woman-on-top positions are excellent for the woman who likes to be in control. By facing away from your man, not only can you indulge in your own fantasies, but the sight of your buttocks can be highly arousing for him.*

▲ *Knowing each other's unique and individual needs will increase your chances of achieving simultaneous orgasm.*

whether a change of position is called for and will adapt .

### WOMAN IN CHARGE
Similarly, a woman who feels her own orgasm will take longer than her partner's can use his body to slow him down by keeping his arousal to a minimum while increasing her own. But, if her partner will take longer than her to come, she can increase his arousal by using her hands and then a woman-on-top position to control the pace.

### DOES IT MATTER?
Nevertheless, simultaneous orgasm is not the be-all and end-all of lovemaking and most loving couples recognize this. For example, on some occasions, the quality of the other's orgasm is of greater importance than their own. It should be seen as a bonus, and lovers should concentrate on giving each other pleasure. Then the quality of orgasms for both partners

will be increased and the lovemaking session will be what it should always be – a shared experience between two lovers.

### THE MAN IN CONTROL
To speed up a woman's responses to your caresses, the quality of foreplay has to be what she likes best. Using words, kisses and caresses – and choosing a position where you are in control – should all help to hurry things up for her.

If you have difficulty holding back your own orgasm, a good idea is to have one first yourself. This is because your second orgasm always takes longer than the first. Obviously, if it is going to leave you temporarily impotent for

▼ *Use your hands and lips on your partner's body as she stimulates her vulval area to bring herself closer to orgasm.*

*THE BEST WAY MY PARTNER AND I FIND OF TIMING OUR ORGASMS IS THROUGH THE WOMAN-ON-TOP POSITION. BY FACING EACH OTHER WE CAN GAUGE EACH OTHER'S LEVEL OF AROUSAL AND TIME OUR ORGASMS PERFECTLY.*

*BECAUSE MY BOYFRIEND COMES VERY QUICKLY ON PENETRATION, IF HE HAS AN EARLIER ORGASM, WE CAN THEN MAKE LOVE AT A PACE WHICH ALLOWS ME TIME TO REACH ORGASM AS WELL.*

◀ *Facing towards your man in this position allows you to see when he is aroused – and vary the pace accordingly.*

any length of time it is not a good idea. But, if this is not the case, in an understanding relationship, your partner will be delighted to give you two climaxes in one lovemaking session, if the quality of her own climax is likely to be improved.

### MAKE THE FOREPLAY GOOD
The choice of position you use for intercourse is important but, as in all lovemaking, excluding quickie sex which has a charm of its own, the quality of foreplay you choose is crucial.

Use your fingers and tongue in a way that will bring her to the brink of orgasm. Tell her what you want to do to her, and how much you want her. If she likes you to use earthy language as you make love, then do so. Gauge from her reactions when to enter her.

### CREATIVE USE OF THE VIBRATOR
If you have a vibrator or dildo, use it over her body but pay special attention to her vulval area. Or get her to use it on herself and then use your hands and lips to please her elsewhere.

Let her use the vibrator in the way she likes best. If she uses it on her clitoris,

▲▶ *As a man usually climaxes before a woman, there are a number of ways he can control the pace so that she can 'catch up with him'.*

▲ *Deep penetration will prevent a man climaxing too soon – it minimizes sensations to the penis.*

▼ *Skilful use of a dildo will soon increase your partner's arousal levels – use your other hand and your lips to caress her.*

use your fingers inside her vagina, or if she prefers to insert the vibrator inside her, then use your fingers or tongue on her clitoris. When she is almost ready to climax, then enter her.

### ENCOURAGE FANTASY

If she likes to fantasize, encourage her to do so. There is no reason why she should not do this as you make love. And for many women, this is a classic way to bring them closer to orgasm as they let their mind roam free.

### GET HER TO MASTURBATE

Because a woman knows her own sexual needs better than anyone, try encourag-

ing her to masturbate. However, you need not be a spectator. Involve yourself by kissing her lips, breasts, thighs, or anus. Then, when she is ready, she can tell you when to penetrate her.

### POSITIONS

For this, it is best to avoid the more athletic positions where you need to concentrate on your own technique rather than your partner's needs.
• Use the missionary position. Lie your partner back, open her legs as wide as possible and enter her. She may prefer to wrap her legs around your waist or perhaps put them over your shoulders so that penetration is deeper.

Start thrusting slowly and encourage her to stimulate her clitoris as you concentrate on timing your orgasm with hers. Be guided by her reactions as to when you should increase the pace. As her orgasm approaches, thrust as hard as possible. Suck her breasts or kiss her lips as you do this.
• Try a side-entry position, which is probably the best position in terms of versatility and ease of access. The man

▶ *Rear entry is ideal for the woman who has a sensitive G spot. He can then thrust toward the front wall of her vagina.*

# CREATIVE LOVING

▶ *In the side-entry position the man can easily stimulate the woman's clitoris. It is, therefore, a good position to control the speed of her orgasm. And although it is a very relaxing position, it also allows a lot of movement for those couples wanting to be more energetic.*

▼ *A rear-entry position has two advantages when trying to increase the woman's level of arousal – she can fantasize more easily and at the same time her partner can stimulate her G spot.*

lies at right angles to his partner's body under her raised and parted thighs. Normally one of the more restful positions, there is no reason why it cannot be used more energetically. The woman is free to caress her clitoris or you can do it for her. It also gives the woman freedom of movement to turn her head towards you so that you can kiss and caress her and see when her orgasm is imminent.

When you have entered her, be guided by her as to how hard you should thrust. Also, use your hands to stimulate her buttocks and anus if she likes.

• Enter her from behind. If she has a sensitive G spot, a rear-entry position allows you to thrust towards the front wall of her vagina. Get her to lie on her front and make sure that she is comfortable. Get her to raise her buttocks as high as she can, so that she is literally offering herself up to you. Use your fingers to part her vaginal lips and enter her. She should be highly aroused and providing her own lubrication. If not, then use saliva on her vulva.

Encourage her to stimulate her clitoris and thrust slowly at first, aiming for her G spot and holding back your own orgasm until she is fully aroused.

### MOVEMENT
In all these positions, many men concentrate almost exclusively on thrusting. But the creative lover can use his penis in other ways during intercourse. Sadly, sideways movement of the penis is often ignored which is a pity because not only is it slightly less arousing to the man, thus giving him more control, it is also highly stimulating for the woman.

So, when your penis is inside her vagina, resist the temptation to thrust all the time and concentrate instead on sideways control. Move your hips and buttocks and try to hit the side walls of your partner's vagina. Then try rotating your penis inside. Experiment to see what she likes best.

### FEMALE LEAD
For many women, it can be highly arousing to dictate the pace of love-making. And for most this involves woman-on-top positions. There are many variations on this theme but the two basic ones involve facing toward

*My boyfriend always seems to come before me during intercourse although he keeps me satisfied in other ways, sexually. Although this bothers him more than me it is beginning to become a problem. How can I help him?*

*When you make love, you need to take charge of what is happening. The best way to do this is to choose one of the woman-on-top positions. In these, you are in charge and what happens is dictated by you and how you use your body. You should be able to determine when your partner has his orgasm and by stimulating yourself, you will be able to have more control over when you have your own orgasm.*

*In turn, he probably needs to spend more time in arousing you. Ensure he does this, but try to discourage him from thinking of it as a problem and get him to see sex with you in a slightly more creative and inventive way.*

whole penis is inside you. You can vary the depth of penetration by arching your back away from him or leaning towards him. If his orgasm is approaching, try moving from side to side so that the friction against his penis is reduced and he becomes less aroused.

Also, research has shown, surprisingly, that the deeper the penetration, the less arousing it is for the man. So, if he looks as if he is going to come too quickly lean forwards, allowing him inside you as deeply as possible.

• Facing away from him. This position has all the advantages of the other woman-on-top positions – except you are unable to see your partner's reactions to what you are doing. However, you can always get him to tell you if his own orgasm is close. The bonus of this position is that you are able to fantasize by looking away from him. Also, you can use your lover's penis in a more uninhibited way.

You can try using it as a starting-off position – as the sight of your buttocks may be particularly arousing to your partner – and as climax approaches, turn around, while keeping your partner's penis inside you. ❤

▲ *Use your mouth and hands on his penis to increase your man's level of arousal.*

▼ *If a woman takes longer to arouse, the man will have to delay his own climax while speeding up hers.*

your lover, or facing away from him.
• Facing him. This position gives you complete freedom to use your hands to explore his body and see him so that you can gauge his reactions. It enables you to set the pace and control the depth and frequency of his thrusting. It also allows you to use your body creatively – up and down and sideways as well as using a kind of grinding motion. Lay your partner down on his back, squat over his penis and use your hands to help him penetrate you.

Start by using slow short strokes, allowing only the top of his penis inside you and then, without increasing the pace, lengthen the strokes so that the

# THE G SPOT

*Making the most of the G spot can add a whole new dimension to a couple's lovemaking. It can also provide men and women with powerfully different types of orgasm.*

Until the 1970s, it was thought that women were almost entirely aroused to climax by clitoral stimulation and that men could only have an orgasm if their penis was stimulated.

But there is a hidden area in both men and women that – when stimulated correctly – produces intense excitement and orgasm. For men, this area is the prostate gland; in women, the area is called the G spot. It was in the 1940s that the German obstetrician and gynecologist Ernest Gräfenberg described a 'zone of erogenous feeling...located in the anterior (front) wall of the vagina'. It is this area that has become known as the G (for Gräfenberg) spot. Researchers have now investigated the G spot in more detail.

## FOR HER

In the 1980s, American researchers Beverly Whipple and John Perry discovered that if this area is properly stimulated, the result can be intensely satisfying orgasm, and that if these orgasms do occur, women will very often ejaculate a small amount of clear fluid. Analysis revealed that this fluid is similar in composition to the seminal fluid from the male prostate gland.

Such findings were initially thought to be unbelievable by those who insisted that the clitoris was the source of female pleasure. But Whipple and Perry examined 400 women volunteers and every one was found to have a G spot, which seems to indicate that this hidden pleasure center is not the exception, but the rule, among women.

### WHAT IS IT?

The G spot appears to be a small cluster of nerve endings, glands, ducts and blood vessels around the urethra – the urinary passage running in front of the vaginal wall.

It cannot normally be felt when it is unaroused, only becoming distinguishable as a specific area during deep vaginal stimulation.

When this happens, it begins

to swell, sometimes very rapidly indeed, and a small mass with distinct edges stands out from the vaginal wall.

Because the fluid ejaculated during a G spot orgasm is very similar to the prostatic fluid (only without sperm), many scientists believe that the G spot is a rudimentary version of the male prostate gland.

### WHERE IS IT?

Lying approximately halfway between the pubic bone and the cervix, within an inch of either side of an imaginary line drawn vertically down from the navel, the G spot is not the easiest part of the female anatomy to find. The problem is that it has to be stimulated to be found, and found to be stimulated.

### FINDING THE G SPOT

It is a good idea for a woman to learn where her G spot is, if only to show herself that she does have one. She cannot do this lying down, since gravity tends to pull the internal organs away from the vaginal entrance. A sitting or squatting position is preferable. It is probably bet-

*◄ Using one of the many woman-on-top positions allows the woman to control the direction and depth of the penis, giving direct stimulation to her G spot and providing an exquisitely intense orgasm.*

ter for her to begin her search for the G spot while sitting on the lavatory. This is because deliberate stimulation of the G spot often causes an initial sensation that feels like a desire to urinate. If the woman makes sure that she has passed water first, but remains on the lavatory, she will gain an added sense of security.

### USE BOTH HANDS

Using her finger, she should then apply a firm upward pressure to the front of the internal vaginal wall. It may help if she presses firmly down on the outside of her tummy with the other hand.

The G spot should now begin to swell, and will feel like a small lump between the fingers inside and outside the vagina. Although, on average, the G spot appears to be about the same size as a dime, there is no real norm – and nor does size seem to have anything to do with the sensation produced.

As the G spot continues to be stroked, pleasurable contractions begin to sweep through the uterus. Ultimately, a deep orgasm will be experienced that will feel totally different from one

*"NOW THAT MY HUSBAND HAS DISCOVERED HOW TO STIMULATE MY G SPOT WHEN WE MAKE LOVE, MY ORGASMS HAVE BECOME INCREDIBLY INTENSE – FAR BETTER THAN ANY I'VE EXPERIENCED BEFORE."*

caused by clitoral stimulation. At this point, the woman may ejaculate a small amount of clear fluid from the urethra. Contrary to what she may feel, this is not urine.

Once a woman has become used to these sensations, she can continue to experiment while kneeling with her knees apart on the floor or bed.

### JOINT DISCOVERY
Of course, a sympathetic partner can make the discovery of a woman's G spot far more intimate and enjoyable.

In this case, the woman should lie face down on the bed with her hips raised by one or two pillows. Her partner can then gently place two fingers inside her and begin to stroke the front of the vaginal wall.

By moving her pelvis back and forth, the woman can help locate the G spot and also discover the most enjoyable kind of stimulation. The main point to remember is that the initial sensations felt are not those of a desire to urinate. In time, the woman will learn that these

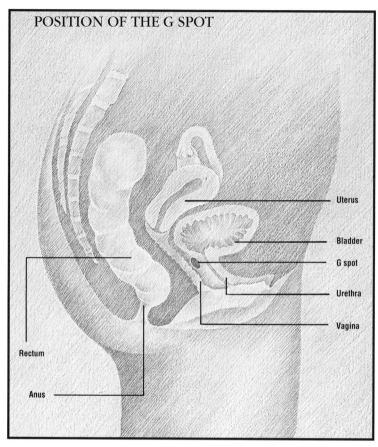

**POSITION OF THE G SPOT**

Uterus
Bladder
G spot
Urethra
Vagina
Rectum
Anus

*I have terrific orgasms from my G spot when my husband penetrates me from behind but it annoys me that I can't get them when I masturbate. Ordinary clitoral orgasms seem so tame by comparison that I'd like to be able to do better. Is there any way around this problem?*

*Obviously your fingers can't reach or you wouldn't be in this dilemma. You could try using a vibrator (not necessarily switched on) or a dildo to stimulate your G spot. These objects will also mimic your husband's penis by stretching your vaginal opening and this too could make them more successful.*

feelings are simply part of the run-up to vaginal orgasm.

### THE IMPORTANCE OF POSITION
Alone among world cultures, Europeans appear to regard the missionary position as being the proven, natural way to make love. A number of other cultures see it as just another, possibly quaint, method – and certainly not one calculated to totally satisfy the female partner.

In the missionary position, the penis is usually aimed at the rear vaginal wall. This can provide clitoral stimulation, but does not excite the G spot.

Probably the two easiest positions with which to achieve G-spot stimulation are the rear-entry and woman-on-top methods.

Rear-entry love-

▶ *If the woman takes up a position where her hips are supported by one or two pillows, her partner can use his fingers to lovingly stroke her G spot, kissing her at the same time.*

making allows the man's erect penis to stimulate the G spot on the front wall of the vagina – particularly if the woman moves her hips back and forth, so that she can direct her lover's penis to the most pleasurable spot.

### WOMAN ON TOP

Woman-on-top positions also afford direct stimulation of the G spot, and allow the woman to control the direction and depth of the penis. If the man lies on his back, with the woman straddling his erect penis, she can guide his penis to the place that feels best.

The man can help by moving his body and pressing on the base of his penis to make sure the head makes full contact. The result can be a series of intense orgasms for both partners.

Men also have a sort of G spot. Located around the urethra at the neck of the bladder, it is called the prostate gland and, unlike the female G spot, has a well defined function. The prostate gland helps produce the fluid that carries the sperm into the vagina when a couple are having intercourse.

Many men have discovered that stimulation of the prostate gland prior to, or during, intercourse results in an orgasm of unparalleled intensity.

The way in which the man ejaculates is different too. After prostate stimulation, he ejaculates in a gentle flow, rather than in spurts.

### FINDING THE PROSTATE
It is difficult for a man to reach his prostate gland himself, since to do so, he has to insert a finger – or thumb – into his rectum. But it is possible to reach it. The best position is if he lies on his back with his knees bent and drawn up towards his chest.

If he inserts a thumb into his anus, and presses against the front rectal wall, he should be able to feel his prostate – it is a firm mass about the size of a walnut.

As with the female G spot, the discovery of this hidden pleasure center is usually more enjoyable if it is shared with a loving partner.

### STIMULATING YOUR PARTNER
If a woman wants to stimulate her partner in this way, here are a few tips:

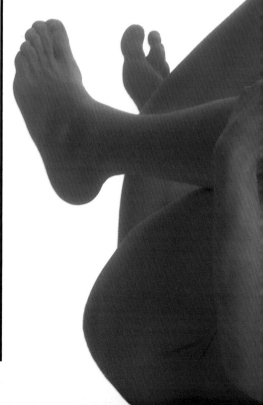

### POSITION OF THE G SPOT

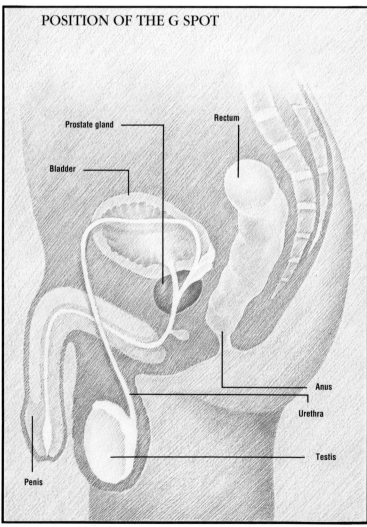

Prostate gland

Bladder

Rectum

Anus

Urethra

Testis

Penis

▼ *The best position for his partner to stimulate his prostate is for the man to lie down with his knees drawn back towards his chest. When the man puts his penis inside the woman, she will be free to use one hand to stimulate his G spot.*

• Make sure your fingernails are not long, as you could damage him inside.
• Ensure that your finger is well lubricated. Unlike your vagina, the anus is not a naturally lubricating organ. Saliva is usually not good enough – you will need to use KY jelly or some other similar lubricant.
• Lie him down on the bed on his back and slowly, gently insert a finger into his anus. Wait for a few seconds as he becomes accustomed to your finger being there. Do not forget that his bottom may not be used to having things put into it – unlike your vagina.
• Feel up the frontal rectal wall until you find his prostate gland, then massage it firmly.
• Even if you do not touch his penis, he will probably become erect and have an orgasm. ❤

*Some positions seem to give my girlfriend a great deal more pleasure than others and she seems to have really intense orgasms. Why should this be so?*

*Obviously the easiest way for a man to put his penis into a woman's vagina is straight in, so that the length of the penis is parallel with the vaginal walls. Yet, because of the variation of sensation that a woman is capable of feeling, it makes sense to vary the angle of approach. It may well be that your girlfriend has a sensitive G spot and when you use a position where your penis comes into contact with the front wall of her vagina, this is when she has her most intense orgasms. Try stimulating her G spot and bring her to orgasm this way, then she can compare the sensations.*

" *I BECOME INCREDIBLY AROUSED AND ACHIEVE MARVELLOUS ORGASMS WHEN MY PROSTATE IS MASSAGED. IF MY GIRLFRIEND FELLATES ME AT THE SAME TIME, I AM IN ABSOLUTE ECSTASY – IT IS THE MOST WONDERFULLY SEXY FEELING.* "

# 4

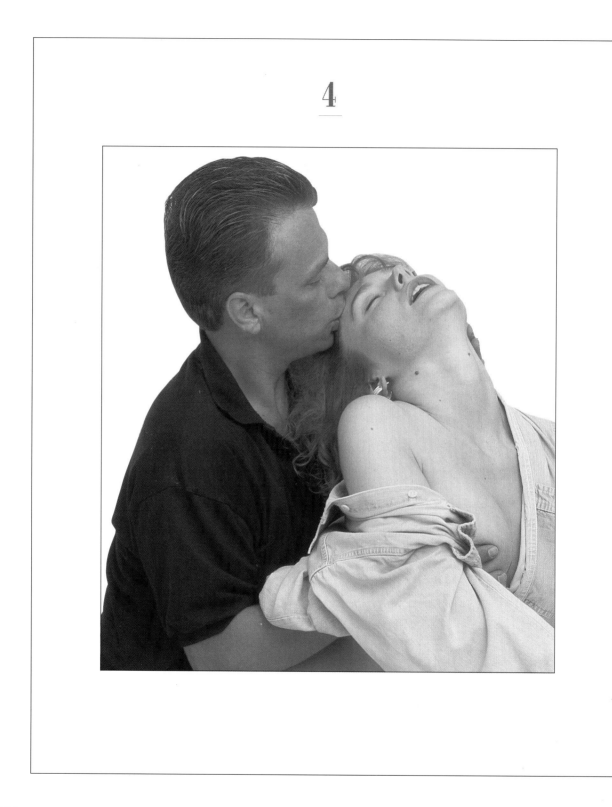

# Enjoying Sex

Sex is such an intense experience that it is hardly surprising that human beings have invented all sorts of ways to increase and prolong the pleasure. The brain is the most powerful organ of all when it comes to our sex lives, and experienced lovers at every period of history, and in every culture, have enjoyed thinking up new methods to stimulate their partners. If you are experiencing the intensity of a new relationship, or if you have been with your partner for a while and want to inject new excitement into your love life, this chapter is for you.

# IMAGINATIVE LOVEMAKING

*Predictability may be valued in certain areas of life but, when it come to sex, experimenting with new techniques is always a bonus.*

▼ *The advanced lover knows his or her – and their partner's – limits and weaknesses and exploits them in their sexual lives together.*

Lovemaking may be infinitely variable, according to the 'experts', but for most couples there comes a time when they crave for something a little novel. And, however satisfactory their orgasms are, they long for a way to make their lovemaking particularly memorable.

Exploring variations of their usual lovemaking techniques can open up new options.

Sex can be mundane or satisfactory – it can also be relaxed, slow and sensual, quick and explosive, athletic and exciting – even bizarre. It is up to us to decide what we want.

## THE MALE RESPONSE

The male sexual response is much more rapid than the woman's. A man can become aroused and ejaculate in minutes – and if a woman's clothes, body, smell and touch arouse him sufficiently, he may orgasm almost immediately.

For unlike women, a man needs 'positive sex'. In other words, he cannot be made love to passively because he must have an erection. Yet, there can be times when his sexual experi-

> *My partner and I have always enjoyed sensual massage prior to lovemaking. In the past we simply used our hands and lots of oil, but we have now widened our repertoire to include the use of ice, feathers – even rubber gloves! The different sensations can be highly erotic!*

ence needs some modifying. So, both the man's imagination and the woman's inventive use of it can be the most valuable sex aid of all.

### THE WOMAN'S RESPONSE

The woman's response is much more varied than the man's. Because of this, it is not surprising that so many women find that much of their sexual resources remain untapped. The golden rule for the man is to remember that his partner's sexual needs are unique. The wise lover listens and learns and the key requisite to a varied and fulfilling sex life for both partners is an open mind.

### NOVELTY

Even for the couple who like predictability in their sex lives, a favorite position or technique can be transformed if it is practiced in a different venue or in a slightly different way. What follows are suggestions to perk up a couple's existing sexual favorites.

### USING CLOTHES

Almost everyone finds clothes exciting

sexually from time to time, although men are more easily aroused visually than women. So, for men particularly, a sexily-clad partner can have a dramatic effect on the intensity of their orgasms.

Just wearing suspenders and stockings and getting her partner to use 'quickie' rear-entry sex can turn the routine nature of a position into something new. Perhaps clothes represent a kind of restraint which may help to explain their sexual appeal. Certainly oral sex for both partners can be much more arousing for some couples if one of them is partially clothed.

### BONDAGE

Bondage is the gentle art of tying up your lover. The idea is not to make your partner do something that they would not do unrestrained. It is to enable one partner to tease the other until they almost beg to be brought to orgasm. So, the sex repertoire of the advanced couple can be greatly enhanced.

There are dangers, however. The couple should have a pre-arranged signal that means 'release me'. Knots should never

▲ *Pamper your partner – let him lie back relaxed while you bring him to a climax. Use your hands to arouse him and then, when you think the time is right, use your mouth to give him a memorable orgasm.*

*107*

**FEMORAL INTERCOURSE**

THIS IS ANOTHER WAY TO ORGASM FOR THE MAN THAT CAN BE USED OCCASIONALLY. ORIGINALLY EMPLOYED AS A METHOD OF BIRTH CONTROL OR A MEANS OF PRESERVING VIRGINITY, THE MAN PRESSES HIS PENIS BETWEEN HIS PARTNER'S CLOSED THIGHS AND EJACULATES BETWEEN THEM. THE PENIS SHOULD BE PLACED NEAR THE TOP OF THE THIGHS SO THAT THE SHAFT GOES IN BETWEEN HER LABIA AND SHE IN TURN PRESSES HARD DOWN ON IT. SOME WOMEN SAY THAT IT CAN GIVE A KEENER SENSATION THAN ACTUAL PENETRATION. ALMOST ANY POSITION CAN BE USED – PROVIDED THE WOMAN CAN PRESS HER THIGHS TOGETHER.

▲ *Even the slightest variation on a favorite technique in terms of position, or even time and place, can add a new and exciting slant to lovemaking that has become something of a routine.*

tate this, but it is always worth trying to make love at different times of the day and in different places.

And it does not always have to be full intercourse. A caress, oral sex or even quickie sex can all be highly arousing and need not take much time. The couple who are in tune with each other's own unique needs always find the time and the place to make love.

### EROTIC VIDEOS
Erotic videos have their place too. Apart from making your own video, you can watch one together and mimic what is happening on the screen. So, if the man is performing cunnilingus on the woman, so too can the man watching do it to his partner. The video can even be put on hold.

### MASSAGE
Sensual massage is a tried and tested means of arousal. But there are variations that advanced lovers can find exciting and stimulating.

•Feathers. The use of feathers on either partner's body as a means of arousal can be a tantalizing and highly erotic experience. Use them as you would use your hands during a conventional sensual

be too tight, nothing should ever be tied round the neck, and gags should also be quick-release. The dangers for the couple who trust each other, though, are minimal.

### BLINDFOLDS
A blindfold, provided it is not tied too tight, can provide unique sensations in even the most tried and tested lovemaking techniques. This is because if we do not use our eyes, the remaining senses tend to be magnified to compensate.

### DIFFERENT TIMES OF THE DAY
The most common time and place for making love is late at night – and usually in bed. Inevitably, practicalities dic-

> *I have a vibrator but would like my boyfriend to use it on me when we make love. Are there any variations on its use?*
>
> *One variation is simply for the woman to vary her position and mix vibrator use with creative use of the man's hands and mouth. So, if the woman goes on all fours, the man can get underneath her, and use his tongue on her clitoris while inserting the vibrator inside her.*
>
> *Another variation is for the man to enter her from behind while she uses the vibrator on her clitoris. The permutations are many. And for the bottom-orientated woman, dual vibrating devices can be inserted in her anus and vulva.*

massage, leaving the genitals until last.
•Ice. This has a curiously shocking effect which some lovers find highly stimulating. You should let it melt a little so that there are no square corners – ice straight from the freezer could damage the skin. Use it to trace a path all over your partner's body.

### SEXUAL GAMES

For the couple who want to increase their erotic repertoire, here are a few sensual games that they may like to play, bearing in mind that they are designed only as starting points.

### HIM – FOR HER

Get your partner to lie back on the bed and make herself comfortable. Use dressing-gown cord or something similar to tie her feet and hands gently together. Then use oil on her body to give her an all-over massage, without touching her genitals. Use your penis to excite her, perhaps by tracing a path along her body. Allow her to kiss your penis and take it into her mouth. But remember, it is the quality of her orgasm you are after – not your own.

Now facing towards her feet, place your knees either side of her and use your tongue on her clitoris, using gentle strokes. As she becomes more aroused insert

▶ *In lovemaking, there is a time to be selfish and a time to give. With a little imagination and sensitivity to your partner's needs, even masturbation can take on new dimensions.*

one or more fingers inside her. Then, as her orgasm approaches, reduce the pace until it subsides. How often you do this is up to you, but the idea is to make her orgasm memorable. You can complete the experience with your hands and mouth, or you can enter her yourself.

### HER – FOR HIM

Get your partner to lie back while you tie his feet and hands together. Massage him, ignoring his genitals and

*◄ By knowing what is available, a couple can accept or reject lovemaking techniques – or even adapt them to their own preferences.*

*▼ Light restraint, using loose bonds, can be highly erotic. Choose a position where you can see each other, take things gently and always have a prearranged 'release' signal.*

then when he is aroused and has a firm erection, face away from him and kneel so that your vulva is close to his face and your mouth to his penis. Lightly brush your vulva against his lips and take his penis in your mouth. Grasp the root of his penis with your hands and build up a slow rhythm, all the time increasing the pressure on his lips as you move from side to side.

As his orgasm approaches, stop and concentrate on using your body to excite him, keeping the pressure on his lips from your vulva and perhaps using your breasts to tease him. Then, when

you sense the time is right, take his penis into your mouth and start again, increasing the pace and pressure. It is up to you how often you repeat this stage. Then, when he can take no more, raise the tempo. Suck hard on his penis as you take it into your mouth as deeply as you can and move your head up and down, while using your hand to masturbate him until he comes.

## SPANKING
Men seem to enjoy spanking more than women, although it plays an impor-

tant part in some couples' sexual repertoire. Like bondage, it should never be allowed to get out of hand.

For the man to spank the woman, it is probably best done when she is draped over his knee as he gently smacks her buttocks. The man can use his other hand, perhaps to stroke her clitoris or even insert his finger inside her vulva.

For the man who knows the finger and thumb technique – inserting one or more fingers inside her vagina, perhaps stroking her G spot as he uses his thumb on her clitoris – the extra dimension of smacking her raised buttocks can be highly memorable for both partners.

And for the man, having his buttocks spanked is more erotic if he raises them. The intensity of sensations can be dramatically increased for him by alternating between squeezing and parting his buttocks and smacking them while masturbating him at the same time.

## POSTILLIONAGE

Postillionage, inserting a finger in your partner's anus, can be highly erotic. The only danger is that bacteria lurk inside the anus so a man should never transfer his fingers from the anus to the vulva. For the same reason, the woman should not use postillionage on her partner and then masturbate him.

Position is all-important for this, so it is best if the recipient goes on all fours. For the man, this means that access to his prostate, or G spot, is possible and the woman can use her finger to give him this type of orgasm alone.

For her, postillionage is best in conjunction with intercourse – probably with

*▼ When it comes to actually finding new ways for both partners to use their imagination to enjoy sex to the full, the possibilities are almost endless.*

the man on top. If she raises her legs and clasps them around his waist – or better still his neck – the man can choose his moment and, as orgasm approaches, insert a finger into her anus.

For both sexes, KY jelly should be used on the finger to make entry to the anus as comfortable as possible.

## KISSING THE PERINEUM

For men and women, the perineum is delightfully sensitive, and unique sensations can be provided by running your tongue along the crevice between your partner's buttocks. It is best if the receiver lies face down on the bed, perhaps with a couple of pillows placed underneath their stomach.

The kissing and licking of the perineum can also be used along with masturbation. It is probably best not to indulge in oral sex afterwards. And it is a good idea for the giver to use a mouthwash afterwards. ♥

# MAKING LOVE LAST LONGER

*Do you hurry in love? Is your sex life active but short? Then it is time to take measures to make your love last longer.*

There are times in a sexual relationship when 'quickie' sex can be exciting, and times when extended sexual intercourse is required.

Sensuous, prolonged intercourse can not only express an emotional commitment, it can also be far more physically satisfying than a quickie as both partners use all their love and skills to bring each other slowly to a peak of arousal.

Prolonged lovemaking is not an end in itself. The key is to share your thoughts and reactions and to be sensitive to your partner's needs and feelings.

Arousal can start long before sexual intercourse begins. It can be triggered by sensual kisses and caresses – and also by a wide range of other stimuli. Daydreaming about your lover or a fantasy figure, hearing a certain song, smelling an evocative scent, tasting particular food or drink – can all put you in the mood for love.

If you want to prolong lovemaking, the best way is to extend not only the experience itself, but both the lead-up and follow-on to lovemaking.

### STAGES OF AROUSAL

Both men and women experience the same set of responses to sexual arousal.

The first stage is excitement. It can last from three minutes to many hours, and can be brought on by physical or emotional stimuli – kissing, caressing, or

▶ *Anticipation is an important part of sexual arousal. Even the act of undressing can be highly arousing, although it is a part of foreplay that is often overlooked, especially by women, in their excitement.*

▼ *Some people make the mistake of believing that the ability to last in bed makes them good lovers. If both partners are not actually enjoying the experience, however, then it is likely to prove an empty one.*

just by thinking about the object of your desires. The man's penis and nipples, and the woman's clitoris, breasts, nipples and labia, will engorge with blood.

In the second stage, or plateau, a flush spreads across their bodies and the engorged parts further swell and darken in color.

Once plateau is reached, orgasm usually follows after a half to three minutes. This is then followed by resolution, when tissue returns to its normal size and color.

In women, orgasm can be followed by a return to the plateau phase and multiple orgasms, while men often need a period of at least 20 minutes to a day to recover, before attempting further intercourse.

### STRIPPING FOR ACTION

There is nothing quite as exciting as the taking off of clothes in preparation for making love. But women can make the mistake of stripping too quickly – a pity, since

▲ *Take turns to massage each other, telling your partner exactly what you find the most pleasurable.*

▼ *The skin is a highly sensitive area. Try licking your partner all over to find his or her most pleasurable areas.*

*I've heard that holding back from ejaculation is harmful, and so I'm not happy about trying to prolong lovemaking. Is this true?*

*Like menstruation, ejaculation is surrounded by many myths and taboos. Many societies believe that semen is imbued with a man's spirit and strength. For this reason, Arabian, Indian and Oriental love manuals all encouraged 'Imsak', or ejaculation control, and interpret the feeling of sleepiness after emission as a sign that a man is weakened by the act. In modern western society, in trying to reassure people that sex is a normal and harmless pastime, people went to the opposite extreme – propounding that not indulging in sexual activity is harmful.*

*During lovemaking, the genitals of both sexes become engorged with blood. After orgasm, they return to normal within 10-15 minutes. But if orgasm does not happen, the process of 'resolution' can take up to half a day and leave you feeling bruised and unsatisfied. However unpleasant it feels, though, no permanent damage is done.*

*MY BOYFIREND AND I FIND THAT THE ANTICIPATION OF INTER-COURSE IS HIGHLY EXCITING FOR THE PAIR OF US, SO WE TRY TO DRAW IT OUT AS LONG AS POSSIBLE WITH REMARKS AND GLANCES BEFORE WE EVEN GO NEAR EACH OTHER! BY THIS POINT WE ARE BOTH HIGHLY AROUSED.*

most men find the sight of a partially clad woman extremely arousing.

## THE LANGUAGE OF LOVE
Voice is as important as hands or lips. You can give just as much pleasure by telling them how much you love them, how their body gives you pleasure and how skillful they are.

Before sexual intercourse, try taking a shower or bath together. Not only will you smell and feel good, but you will find

▲ *Oral sex is enjoyed by more than half of sexually active couples. It is an extremely intimate act and as such is valued as a sign of generosity and caring between partners.*

▼ *Nobody should force their partner to have oral sex if it is difficult for them, but in the slow, leisurely build-up to prolonged intercourse, many couples find themselves kissing and sucking their partner's genitals quite naturally.*

that the water, soap and shampoo will help your hands glide easily over your partner's body.

## SLOWING DOWN THE PACE
Skin, with its textures, scent and sensitivity to temperature, is the largest non-genital sexual organ. Yet men, who are less sensitive to touch than women, often ignore this.

The woman can gently rub and squeeze her man's penis and testicles, particularly the glans or head and the frenulum or ridge of tissue on the underside of the glans, and the man can exert gentle pressure or friction on the woman's clitoris.

Most women find it exciting to have their partner insert his second finger into their vagina, with the palm pressed against the mount of Venus, and the first finger doubled over. By gently moving his hand, her clitoris is stimulated directly with the knuckle of his first finger.

As intercourse begins, make sure that the excitement phase continues for as long as possible. Watch and listen to each other's reactions and, above all, tell your partner when excitement builds too far, so you can hold back.

## THE KEY TO SENSUAL FOREPLAY
The mouth is highly responsive. Second only to the genitals on the sensitivity scale, and with greater mobility, it offers

▼ *Taking a shower together is an excellent way for couples to get to know each other's bodies before intercourse.*

## DID YOU KNOW?

### KISSING TIPS

KISSING SHOULD NOT BE RESTRICTED TO MOUTH-TO-MOUTH CONTACT. THE MOUTH IS PERFECTLY EQUIPPED TO FEEL AND TASTE EVERY CREASE AND CREVICE OF THE BODY, AND BODY KISSES ARE ESSENTIAL COMPONENTS OF FOREPLAY. TONGUE CARESSES OF THE CALVES, KNEES AND THIGHS CAN ACT AS A TANTALIZING PRELUDE TO INTERCOURSE – CONVENTIONAL OR ORAL. THE WISE LOVER SHOULD NEVER BE IN A HURRY.

• DO NOT GIVE WET, MESSY KISSES. YOU SHOULD NORMALLY SWALLOW BEFORE KISSING, BUT MAKE SURE THAT YOU DO ANYWAY

• DO NOT GO ON AND ON WITH THE SAME KISS FOR TOO LONG. ONE OF YOU MIGHT GET BORED. RING THE CHANGES BY TRYING DIFFERENT SORTS OF KISSES

• DO NOT GIVE LOOSE-LIPPED, SLOPPY KISSES. IT ALWAYS FEELS BETTER TO HAVE A FIRM MOUTH AGAINST YOURS

• DO KEEP YOUR MOUTH IN TIP-TOP CONDITION. POORLY KEPT TEETH AND SMELLY BREATH ARE A REAL TURN-OFF, AND AN INSULT TO YOUR LOVER

• DO MAKE SURE THAT YOU AND YOUR LOVER EAT THE SAME STRONGLY FLAVORED FOODS AT THE SAME TIME! GARLIC CAN BE UNPLEASANT

• DO VISIT A DENTIST REGULARLY, CLEAN YOUR TEETH THOROUGHLY AND FREQUENTLY USE AN ANTISEPTIC MOUTHWASH TO KEEP YOUR BREATH FRESH

• DO KEEP LIPS SOFT AND SMOOTH WITH LIP SALVE OR CREAM

a variety of pleasures. With the potential enjoyment to be derived from oral contact, kissing techniques are clearly of great importance in lovemaking.

### THE IMPORTANCE OF TECHNIQUES

Kissing your lover's erogenous zones is the most intimate and stimulating act of foreplay. Start by kissing the feet. Then stretch the palms of your lover's hands taut, and lick and kiss them all over.

Attack the responsive area behind the knees with forceful kisses. Continue up the legs to the inside of the thighs.

Put your face right against your lover's thigh as you press your lips down. Sink your mouth into the buttocks with sharp, strong kisses. Trace the spine with your tongue, alternating soft kisses with firm kisses on the back of the neck, and nuzzling the earlobes.

A woman's breasts are most sensitive to oral caresses. A man should try sucking the tip of her nipple sensually and then pushing as much of her breast into his mouth as possible, taking the nip-

> *MY BOYFRIEND HAS A TENDENCY TO GET OVER-EXCITED AND COME TOO QUICKLY. BUT I CAN CONTROL HIS PASSION BY USING THE WOMAN-ON-TOP POSITION.*

▲▼ *Side by side is the perfect position between the man on top and the woman on top. It keeps rhythm constant and saves wrenched muscles when you change position.*

ple gently in his teeth and flicking his tongue backwards and forwards across its hardened tip.

Several lovemaking positions help you maintain intercourse for long periods. All rely on giving the woman control of movement. Generally, the aim is to slow down the male, because while a woman can experience several orgasms and still enjoy intercourse, once the man has 'come' that stage of lovemaking for him is over for a while.

If the man seems to be entering the plateau phase the woman can withdraw his penis and stop ejaculation by placing her thumb on his frenulum, with her index and middle finger on the other side of the penis, and gently squeezing.

### THE WOMAN ON TOP
Here, the man lies on his back and the woman sits astride. She can sit upright

or lie full length on him, with her legs outside or inside his. By pressing a hand on the small of her back, this position stimulates the clitoris by compressing his penis between their bodies and allowing her freedom to move. Her partner can caress her breasts and stroke her back and buttocks while she moves.

### THE LAP OF LUXURY
Here, the man sits on a bed with his legs stretched out. His partner lowers herself into his lap, stretches her legs over his and, providing both partners are ready, takes his penis into her vagina.

She can wrap her legs around his back, or relax with her legs stretched out on either side of him.

Both can sit back, supporting themselves on their hands, or she can cling around his neck. He can also sit in her lap, with his legs over hers or wrapped around her back.

In a further variation, he can double his legs under so he is in a kneeling position, and she can lie back.

*We love to relax completely and make love for hours – but we have two teenage children in the house. What do you suggest?*

*There are two strategies that can be suggested. The first is to teach your children the value of privacy and of 'adult time'. Make it clear that there are times when you want to be left alone in peace and cannot be interrupted (unless in emergencies). The second strategy is to arrange for times when you are alone in the house. Encourage them to have outside pursuits to give you time with each other.*

By raising one knee and resting her foot against his chest, she can control his thrusts by rocking her foot against him. He, in turn can kiss and caress her foot – a very erotic action for many women.

Whichever variation is chosen, since both man and woman are limited in their movements, lovemaking can be slow and gentle and go on for as long as the couple wish.

### SIDE BY SIDE

A particularly relaxing position is 'side by side'. The woman can rest on her partner's thigh, or vice versa. Movement is restricted and so this position is ideal for slow, leisurely love.

In this position, both are able to use a hand to caress the other and can exchange long looks and kisses. Side by side is an ideal 'resting' position, which you can roll over into and use as a means of slowing down excitement.

### HOW TO MOVE

Movements are usually 'in and out' thrusting, and it is these that primarily stimulate the man by rubbing the glans and shaft of his penis. However, the clitoris can be equally stimulated by side-to-side and swirling motions. These can be highly exciting to the woman, while her partner is kept on 'hold'.

▲ *Sitting in each other's laps allows complete visual contact with both hands free to explore each other's bodies.*

▼ *Kissing should not just be on the mouth. It is also a perfect, sensuous way to explore every part of the body.*

And, of course, the best end to love-making is the gradual build up to, and explosion of, orgasm.

### CHOOSING YOUR MOMENT

Before embarking on a long, slow session of sex you must both be in the mood for it at that particular time.

We all have our different rhythms. Many women are very easily aroused at the time they ovulate or during their menstrual periods, while others find sex less enticing in the week before their period starts. Tiredness, worry or even cold weather can put people off. However, the best time is during holidays and weekends when you have more time to devote to each other.

Make sure you have the time, warmth and comfort and privacy. Fit a lock on your bedroom door and take the phone off the hook. Sometimes we are conditioned to hurry sex because of early experiences when we were afraid of being interrupted by parents or flat-mates. We may need to consciously teach ourselves to take it slowly. ❤

# QUICKIE SEX

*For much of their sex lives together, lovers concentrate on a sensual, lingering build-up to lovemaking. Yet sometimes a raw sense of urgency takes over, and then a couple just can't wait...*

Some couples see sex as a ritual. They make love in a predictable way, even on an appointed night of the week. This can be fine for certain people, but others may complain of boredom or look elsewhere for sex in actuality or in fantasy. But why bother, when you can make sex at home so much better?

### BURNING DESIRE

The joys of quickie sex are often overlooked, even by experienced lovers. We all tend to become obsessed with technique, often forgetting the joy there is to be had in spontaneity. A moment of unbridled passion can bring you more than just intense and passionate pleasure. The urgency can rekindle old, forgotten feelings, and in no time you can be transported back to the early days of your relationship, or even the first hours of your sexual awakening.

With so much advice and freedom of speech on the subject of sex today, couples tend to see themselves as enlightened, which indeed they are compared to previous generations. But the knowledge gained is often at the cost of our more basic instincts, and our primeval powers of seduction.

Creating the right mood for lovemaking is often stated to be the path to heightened pleasure, and generally this is true. But the couple who wait for the mood to be 'right' every time may miss out on all but their self–imposed notions of 'romantic' sex.

▲ *The sensational contrast between naked skin and clothes can heighten pleasure and excitement for both of you, adding to the sense of urgency and desire.*

*M*any of today's couples think of intercourse as something that has to be worked up to gradually and with delicacy. Although this kind of lovemaking is an essential part of an intimate relationship, so too are those unplanned moments when you just feel like having sex with no preparation at all.

## SEX ON LOCATION

- ON THE KITCHEN TABLE
- IN THE BATHROOM AT A FRIEND'S DINNER PARTY
- DURING A WALK IN THE WOODS IN A SECLUDED SPOT
- IN A ROCKING CHAIR
- ON THE BEACH AT NIGHT
- IN AN ABANDONED SHED OR BARN
- OVER THE BACK OF THE SOFA
- ON THE CHILDREN'S SWING-SET IN THE GARDEN

Quickie sex often has a quality all its own. Within the confines of your loving relationship it is neither more nor less worthwhile or trivial than lovemaking which has been carefully considered.

### PASSION PLAY

There are plenty of advantages gained with spontaneous sex. It shows how much you fancy each other on a purely physical basis. Romantic interludes and subtle foreplay are all very well, but there are times when one or both partners really need to be shown that they are wanted by their lovers with urgency, right this minute.

### LIGHT MY FIRE

Some women say that quickie sex is better for them than any other approach. As it is unplanned they can simply be taken over by their man's ardor. In fact, some women only have orgasms during intercourse when the sex is sudden and out of their control. No woman seriously wants to be raped, but most will agree that to be taken forcefully by the man

---

### SPONTANEOUS TIPS

- GENTLY RELEASE ONE BREAST FROM THE WOMAN'S BRA SO IT CAN BE SUCKED AND KISSED AS SHE IS FONDLED.
- INSTEAD OF TAKING HER PANTIES OFF, PULL THEM TO ONE SIDE AND INSERT THE PENIS AROUND THE EDGE.
- UNDO THE MAN'S SHIRT BUTTONS TO REVEAL PART OF HIS CHEST. NOT TOO MUCH – JUST ENOUGH TO INSERT ONE HAND TO CARESS HIM.
- UNZIP HIS FLY INSTEAD OF PULLING HIS TROUSERS ALL THE WAY DOWN FOR A DISCREET QUICKIE.
- MAKE A HABIT OF 'FORGETTING' TO WEAR KNICKERS WHEN YOU FEEL IN THE MOOD.
- WOMEN, WEAR A FRONT-FASTENING BRA FOR EASY ACCESS.

## 'I AM SO HOT FOR YOU...'

THERE ARE MANY CELEBRATED EXAMPLES OF SPONTANEOUS SEX ON THE BIG SCREEN. IN THE HOLLYWOOD SIZZLER 'BODY HEAT', WILLIAM HURT SHATTERS A GLASS DOOR WITH A CHAIR TO REACH THE PANTING KATHLEEN TURNER WHO IS STANDING, FROZEN WITH DESIRE, ON THE OTHER SIDE. WHEN HE FINALLY REACHES HER, SHE GASPS 'JUST DO IT!'

THE THRILLER 'NO WAY OUT' FEATURES KEVIN COSTNER AS A US NAVAL OFFICER AND SEAN YOUNG AS THE MISTRESS OF A RICH POLITICIAN IN A SENSATIONAL SCENE WHERE THE TWO MEET IN THE BACK SEAT OF A HUGE LIMOUSINE. THEY SILENTLY TEAR OFF EACH OTHER'S GORGEOUS EVENING CLOTHES AND MAKE LOVE IN A FRENZY AS THE DAZZLING LIGHTS OF THE CITY FLASH COLORS ONTO THEIR NAKED FLESH.

you love is another matter altogether.

Spontaneous sex is often linked with the risk of being discovered in the act by other people. This risk of discovery can be highly exciting, as a degree of naughtiness is essential for some people to enjoy sex at its best. Quickies in semi-public places – in woods, fields or even your own garden – can build up this naughtiness with a stimulating sense of danger and urgency.

The kinds of positions used during quickies are often very different from those used in bed. Unfamiliar movements and body positions produce new and stimulating sensations, and these are often unrepeatable in a more controlled setting.

### DRESS ME UP 'N' DOWN

Quickies are usually carried out with one or both partners partially dressed. This in itself is highly arousing to many people. The sight of a woman who has simply raised her skirt and bent forward over the kitchen table to reveal her naked thighs and bottom can make even the most weary man ready for sex.

The addition of underwear, and in some cases clothes, can make a big difference to the style and the feel of the lovemaking. Some people are turned on by the touch or look of certain clothes. The silkiness of a dress, the sight of high heels or the feel of a man's jumper against bare skin can be an exciting bonus of quickie sex.

For many people, spontaneous sex is

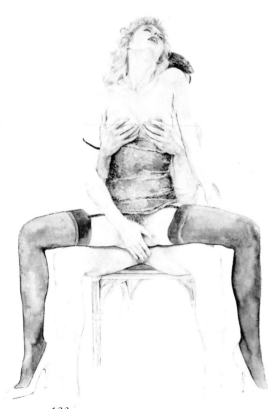

▶ *If the woman is partly dressed while a man makes love to her, it can make her feel especially abandoned and sexy.*

" *SHE COAXED ME INTO THE BATHROOM AT A FRIEND'S DINNER PARTY. I WAS INSTANTLY TURNED-ON, ESPECIALLY WHEN I GUESSED WHAT IT WAS SHE HAD IN MIND – WE MADE PASSIONATE LOVE STANDING AGAINST THE MIRROR. AFTERWARDS WE REALISED NOBODY HAD EVEN MISSED US.* "

a reminder of the days when they were still living with their parents. The chances of any physical contact with boyfriends or girlfriends were minimal in those days, and most young couples became very adept at grabbing the opportunity when they could. While we appreciate the privacy that comes with leaving home, some of the spontaneity and excitement is always lost.

Quickies have other things going for them as well. By not preparing for sex

both partners are unwashed and therefore carry the smell of their sweat and other body fluids on their skin. This earthiness can actually prove to be a real turn on, as the normal act of washing actually removes many of the naturally occurring chemical attractants. Many people, especially men, find their desire heightened by such natural scents.

TAKEN BY STORM

For many people, a quickie is the enactment of a sexual fantasy. Most people have fantasies of taking or being taken by a partner in various strange, unconventional or exotic locations. Quickie sex can achieve this with a little sense of adventure.

Given a choice, and time to think it over, many people would not readily agree to sex in such a place or in that particular way – they would always find

All Photographs Eddison Sadd/Lifetime Vision Ltd

▲ *Why restrain your sex life to the bedroom? An intimate act in a comparatively public place breaks routine and reminds you both of how very special you are to each other.*

some kind of excuse. When it is 'forced' upon them they often greatly enjoy it, and may even then build the event into their future fantasy lives.

Of course, women can take the initiative any time they want, either overtly or in secret – perhaps when they are having a period or need a little time to arouse themselves first. If this is the case for you, why not take a few minutes

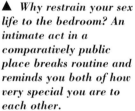

*He came up behind me one day as I was baking in the kitchen. I continued to mix the cake I was making as though nothing unusual was happening. I let him kiss my neck for a while, and then he suddenly pulled my tights down and thrust his penis into my body. It was ecstasy with a twist of vanilla.*

on your own to make sure you're really in the mood, and then go straight for your partner. You can be sure it won't take him long to respond.

Some men are put off the idea of initiating a quickie themselves, because they cannot remember when their partner is having a period, but this

problem is easily solved with a little forethought on the woman's part. After all, many women are most easily aroused during their period and it is a simple matter for the woman to remove her tampon or towel and be ready for sex in a couple of minutes. If the man still has qualms, then just avoid making love on the first heavy day or two or insert a diaphragm ahead of time. This will hold back the flow for a while and allow you to have a 'quickie surprise'.

It is often said that good sex depends on meticulous foreplay to arouse the woman so that her vagina is lubricated. But a woman's vagina can lubricate almost immediately when she is in the mood for quick sex. And some women are most turned on by quickie sex, because of the intense degree of passionate feelings involved.

Sex between true lovers takes many forms and serves many purposes. One of them is that it reinforces their secret bond and by doing so builds up their unique relationship.

In this context, quickies can be especially exciting in the middle of an event at which others are present. Why not take your partner outside the room at a dinner party or other social gathering and make love? You can develop your own private code for letting your partner know that you want them – now.

### ANY TIME, ANY PLACE...

The time and place for quickies can vary endlessly. If you feel in the mood for love, make sure you're wearing clothes through which you're easily accessible – this is obviously easier for women than men, but don't be afraid to use your imagination. Just the act of dressing in this way can make many women feel sexier, and this will be transmitted to their partners through their body language. So, next time you want to show them how much you fancy them, go for it! ❤

# 5

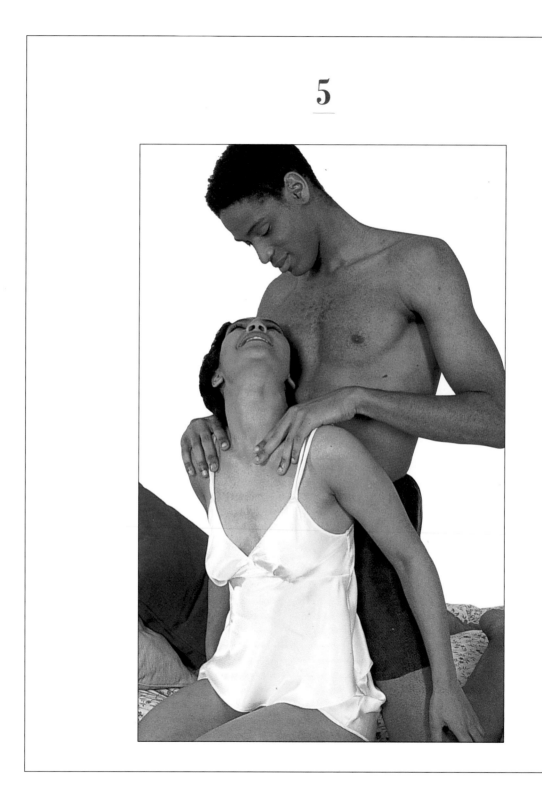

# Sex and Romance

Romance is often part of the beginning of a satisfying sexual relationship, but can fade as lovers become accustomed to each other. Wise couples recognize that sexual habits and patterns do change as a relationship develops, and that although sex may still be important, it becomes less of a driving force with the passing of time. However, sex within a loving context is the most important shared experience any couple can have, so take the trouble to keep romance alive, and you will reap many benefits.

# ROMANTIC SEX

*With a little thought and imagination, any couple can rediscover the early romance that existed in the first weeks of their courtship. And the familiar feelings between them can be used to turn their lovemaking into a memorable experience.*

Most of us understand romance to imply attentiveness, consideration and sensuality in a lover. It conjures up images of being in love when a relationship is new, fresh and exciting. The feelings it creates can be exquisitely insane or they may be agonizing and depressing.

### THE IMPORTANCE OF ROMANCE
Most people who are in a long-term relationship remember wistfully the first days of their courtship. And why not? That was the time when they yearned to be together all the time. Absences were agonizing and the sex – whatever

it may have lacked in finesse – was as frequent as the couple could manage.

The early feelings we have for our partners are indispensable. For most people, they are the basis on which they choose to form their relationships. The love they feel may be the vital ingredient, but that in itself is often a direct result of this early romantic behavior.

### WHEN ROMANCE GOES
Unfortunately, romantic behavior disappears all too quickly in most long-term relationships.

This is not necessarily a bad thing. Most relationships are unable to withstand the dreamy, almost unreal quality on a permanent basis. And as a relationship progresses, the romantic qualities are replaced by something better.

### FROM TIME TO TIME
In an ideal world, the climate would continue to be one where romantic lovemaking goes on all the time. For most of us, however, the practicalities of life mean that we cannot continue in that vein, but the effort made to restore some romance into our relationship will

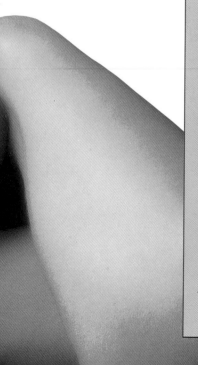

▼ *Most of us start our relationships by being loving and romantic towards our partner. We tend to see our partner through rose-tinted glasses and may credit him or her with qualities we only previously imagined in fantasy.*

---

*I am married to a very good man who provides well for me and the children. He is perfect in many ways but he never behaves in a romantic way or tells me he loves me. I am almost forty now and I am beginning to feel very old and unattractive. Do you think he will change? We have been married almost twelve years.*

*Many men simply do not understand how important it is to a woman to be shown affection and told how attractive she is and how much her partner loves her. You must sit down with your partner and let him know your true feelings.*

be amply rewarded.

For the woman, it means being treated as someone who is cosseted and prized. For the man, it revives his ideas of his masculinity, making him feel someone who is both loved and desired.

For both, a return to romance means a return to more loving behavior, and more frequent, satisfactory sex.

*AFTER ORGASM, MY PARTNER AND I USE THE TIME TO KISS AND CARESS ONE ANOTHER UNTIL WE ARE SUFFICIENTLY AROUSED TO BEGIN LOVE-MAKING ONCE AGAIN.*

### ACT ROMANTICALLY

In a long-term relationship, keeping romance alive can present difficulties after the first flush of enthusiasm.

Yet the couple who are in tune with one another should be able to readily recall the emotions and actions they

▶ *Start your lovemaking at a slow pace; lie close to your lover and gently stimulate her clitoris, telling her of your desire.*

*Quite frankly, I have never had much of a romantic life with my wife, but I greatly enjoy romantic situations with women outside my marriage. Obviously, there's something severely wrong, so what can I do?*

*You probably see romance as a part only of extra-marital activities and feel that you couldn't or shouldn't be romantic with your wife.*

*To some extent, this may be a hangover from your adolescence. You haven't grown up and can't make the level of investment needed to truly love another adult. Your affairs could be a form of adolescent game but they won't bring you lasting happiness, if only because they are so superficial in terms of really knowing and loving another person in a committed way. Perhaps you married too young and are regretting having taken such a step. This kind of situation calls for professional help.*

early courtship. This means finding more time to spend together. A short holiday away, even a day out or perhaps revisiting places that were particularly memorable can be a real tonic.

Always remember birthdays and anniversaries. It is not so much the present that counts, but the fact that you remember. If possible, celebrate them with a meal or an outing.

Be more considerate. Try acting more selflessly – placing a towel on the radiator before your partner has a bath, or bringing an unexpected cup of tea in the morning are both thoughtful acts.

Share activities more. Domestic chores or shared hobbies and sports can be romantic in the right setting. Even painting and decorating can be a shared

used when they first started courting. The familiarity that now exists can be used to good effect. All that is needed is thought and imagination.

Practice the art of surprise. This need not be confined to gifts such as flowers or the occasional present. A meal at a restaurant, or just a specially cooked meal at home, can provide the right atmosphere for love. Candles, a favorite piece of music and a bottle of wine are a good idea for any pair of lovers and set the tone for the evening.

Dress up from time to time. For a man, to see his partner dressed sexily is not just a turn-on, it is flattering as well. It does not have to be overtly sexy, but most men are susceptible to the idea that a woman has dressed specifically for him. For a woman, her man making an effort to look good is a compliment.

Act like lovers. Telephone one another from time to time just to say 'I love you'. Show affection to each other in public. Even something as simple as taking your partner's hand can turn a walk into a romantic episode.

Try to recapture the mood of your

*We have been married for seven years and my husband gives me endless presents. In fact, he's so romantic that it annoys me. What can I do?*

*It sounds as though he could be very insecure. The answer to such behavior usually lies in the man's childhood. He may well have been rejected and now sees you as his only hope for the future.*

*Another possibility is that he is trying, perhaps too hard, to give you an example of how he wants you to behave. Perhaps you don't show enough love to him, or at least not in ways that he wants it to be shown. If this is the problem, a short talk would sort things out. As with all behavior that annoys in marriage, the best course of action is to encourage him when he does what you want, but not to put him down when he doesn't.*

*Perhaps it would make sense for you to find ways that he could please you romantically so that he stops his 'eager puppy' behavior.*

◄ **People who are in a long-term relationship often forget that tenderness is important in romance. Touching and stroking are an end in themselves, and not necessarily a prelude to making love.**

▼ **Show your partner how much you desire him by taking the lead in lovemaking, but choose a position where you are close enough to lean forward and kiss or caress him.**

experience between two lovers if the mood is right.

Touch more. Holding hands or a touch on the shoulder does not need to have any sexual meaning and can often say 'I love you' as fluently as words.

Kiss and cuddle more. Do not be afraid to show each other affection – wherever you may be.

Find new places to make love. Almost any room can be romantic for making love if the mood is

right. But do not confine yourself to indoors. Experiment elsewhere.

## MAKING LOVE ALL DAY

A couple who have been together for any length of time know each other's likes or dislikes and they know exactly what turns the other person on.

Although it is all too easy to fall into the routine of doing only what you know your partner likes, sex and love-making can be much more fun – and more romantic – if both partners explore each other's likes and dislikes, lingering over them, rather than hurrying.

## PREPARING TO LOVE

A long warm bath together always acts as a wonderful prelude to lovemaking. And a romantic alternative to bathing together is for each partner to bathe

the other, soaping them down gently, but leaving the most sensitive of their erogenous zones until last.

### ROMANTIC LOVING – HIM FOR HER

For the man who really wants to go to town, take lighted candles into the bathroom to provide sensual lighting. Prepare the room you intend to make love in beforehand, making sure that it is warm enough and perhaps leaving two glasses of wine by the bed.

Add fragrant oils to the bath as you run the water. Then take your partner into the bathroom and slowly undress her and wash her sensually all over, using plenty of lathery soap.

When you are finished, dry her down thoroughly with a warmed towel, paying loving attention to all of her body from her hands and toes to her breasts and

*AFTER SEVERAL YEARS OF MARRIAGE MY HUSBAND IS AS ROMANTIC AS HE WAS WHEN WE FIRST MET. WE ALWAYS TRY TO MAKE TIME FOR ONE ANOTHER, NO MATTER HOW BUSY WE ARE, AND WE ALWAYS TALK – TO KEEP INTERESTED IN EACH OTHER'S VIEWS.*

▼ *Be attentive to your partner's needs. Romance needs continued interest so talk to your partner about what he or she wants – both in bed and out. Increased interest is flattering and will bring its own rewards.*

bottom. Continue to compliment her, and tell her what you intend to do with her later in the evening.

### MAKE LOVE

When she is dry, pick her up and carry her to the bedroom or wherever you have chosen to make love. If you have provided a bottle of wine, pause while you both take a sip – but not for long.

Kissing, cuddling and prolonged foreplay were habits learned early in courtship, so kiss her all over her body. Then, with her skin tingling from the effects of the bath, apply massage oil all over her body.

### EXPLORE HER BODY

Oral sex is often considered the greatest compliment a lover can pay.

When the oil has been massaged all over her, lay her back and find a position that is comfortable for you. Use your tongue on her clitoris with slow strokes, moving rhythmically the way you both know that she likes best.

### POSITIONS

Any position that allows a couple to gaze at each other and kiss and touch can be romantic. For the man who is spoiling his partner, any of the man-on-top positions are suitable. They allow the man to feel he is in control and he can see and gauge his partner's reactions as they make love.

With your partner lying back on the bed, part her legs gently and enter her. Start off with short, shallow strokes and move slowly at first. Tell her what you want to do and how you want to bring her to orgasm.

ROMANTIC LOVING – HER FOR HIM
Most men love to be bathed. Because your body will be such a turn-on for him, wear as little as possible – a pair of panties, and nothing else. Then undress him, pampering him like a baby. When he is lying in the bath, dangle your breasts over him for a moment, but do not let him touch them. Wash him all over; lather the soap over him, lingering erotically over his penis and his testicles, using soft, upward strokes.

IN BED
Most men find oral sex irresistible. Yet it can be romantic for the woman as well as

◀ *Positions that allow close contact where a couple can observe and communicate with each other help create a feeling of intimacy.*

▼ *Massage your partner with relaxing oil. Rub the oil all over her body. Touch her breasts with light, teasing strokes until she can bear it no longer. Talk to her all the time, telling her what you plan to do.*

she brings her man to the verge of orgasm or if the man comes inside her mouth.

Many men like to know beforehand what is going to happen, so tell him in detail what you are going to do.

Tell him that you are going to nibble his testicles and then lick along the underside of his penis before you take it into your mouth. Next, tell him that you are going to suck him, either to the verge of orgasm or that he can come inside your mouth.

Position yourself comfortably so that he can see what you are doing to him. Then, alternate between just using your mouth and holding the root of his penis with your hand and sucking it with short, firm strokes. ❤

# PLEASING A MAN

*The woman who wants and learns to love her man in an exciting, inventive way will not only turn him on; she will reap rich benefits for herself at the same time.*

▶ *Many women find that if they overcome any natural shyness they feel in making themselves initiate lovemaking, and take the dominant role, their lovers respond and achieve an immensely satisfying and intensely pleasurable climax.*

Modern man has a lot to live up to. Films and TV depict the ideal lover as a virile male with an appetite for sex who knows how to please a woman and who takes pleasure at the same time himself.

He shows few emotions yet he is understanding and strong with an almost infinite capacity to bring his woman to orgasm – usually more than once. Women find him devastatingly attractive and know instinctively how to please him. His body is arousable in a

number of areas but they know that his most sensitive and important area is his genitals or around them.

When a man makes love to a woman he has one principal goal – that of his own orgasm. Of course, he may want to please his partner as well – but his needs are considerably less variable than those of a woman.

But while a man's approach to sex may be more basic and less romantic than a woman's, he still craves love, attention and tenderness as much – if

## PLEASURE SURVEY

IN A MAJOR SURVEY OF MALE SEXUALITY CARRIED OUT IN THE US MEN WERE ASKED WHAT A WOMAN COULD DO TO EXCITE HER PARTNER MORE. IT WAS HOPED THAT THE ANSWERS WOULD HELP WOMEN TO UNDERSTAND MEN AND COMMUNICATE PROPERLY WITH THEM.

WHEN ASKED WHAT A WOMAN COULD DO TO EXCITE HER PARTNER, THE ANSWERS WERE SURPRISINGLY CONVENTIONAL. TO CREATE THE RIGHT ATMOSPHERE FOR MAKING LOVE MEN APPRECIATED:

- DIM LIGHTS AND SOFT MUSIC
- GOOD FOOD
- PERFUME
- PROVOCATIVE CLOTHING
- STRANGE SURROUNDINGS

A FEW MEN PREFERRED AN ATMOSPHERE OF INTRIGUE AND FANTASY BUT MORE MEN WANTED THEIR PARTNERS TO BE NATURAL AND RELAXED. THEY WANTED THEIR PARTNER:

- TO SHOW WARMTH AND AFFECTION
- TO SHOW INTEREST IN THEIR PARTNER
- TO TAKE THE INITIATIVE IN LOVEMAKING
- TO BE RESPONSIVE AND PASSIONATE

perhaps in a different way.

To please a man you do not need any exotic skills or specialist knowledge. If you are to give him a really special time there are a number of preparations you can make.

- Cook him a special meal or have a glass or two of his favorite drinks.
- Wear something sexy that you know he likes.

▼ *Many men enjoy a sexy striptease knowing that it will be followed by a lengthy and passionate lovemaking session.*

*"I LOVE IT WHEN MY GIRLFRIEND TAKES THE LEAD AND THINKS UP SOME NEW AND EXCITING LOVEMAKING POSITIONS. SHE IS AMAZINGLY CREATIVE!"*

• Take a bath or shower together. Many couples, once slightly aroused after kissing and cuddling, like to bathe each other. Do what you find to be the nicest for you as a couple.

• Decide whether you intend to bring him to climax with, or without, full intercourse. This can be a surprise for him but be clear in your own mind of exactly what you intend to do.

• Take responsibility for contraception and tell your partner. Important matters like contraception and 'safer sex' should be discussed fully before making love so that both partners can relax and enjoy their lovemaking.

### LOVE IN ACTION
To please your partner ask him to tell you what he enjoys then use this information

to improve your lovemaking technique.

Surveys show that most men greatly enjoy kissing and cuddling. This may come as a surprise to those women who imagine that men only kiss and cuddle to please them.

As well as his mouth, kiss his ears – put your tongue inside and move it around – eyes, neck, anywhere on his body (except, initially, his genitals). Massage him if he enjoys this or just stroke him in the places he likes best.

### HIS SENSITIVE AREAS

This is a learning process, of course. But the more you take the initiative in sex and explore his body and reactions, the quicker you will discover what areas are the most sensitive and what he really likes having done.

At the same time you will find out which areas to avoid and what (if anything) turns him off. But to avoid this period of trial and error being too long, why not sim-ply ask him to whisper in your ear what exactly he really likes?

### TALK TO HIM

Tell him how wonderful his penis is. The vast majority of men harbor some vestige of phallic inferiority complex, and having their woman tell them it is beautiful, large or hard can be marvellously reassuring – however sophisticated he may be.

Once you are actually in bed together and you are both becoming aroused you will want to set about giving him the most pleasure. For him this will center on his penis and genital area.

Learning how best to handle a man's penis takes time. The best source of information is your partner, so ask him what he likes and then do as he says. Learning how to stimulate his penis properly can turn an ordinary lovemaking session into a memorable one.

▲ *It takes practice to become good at oral sex. Experienced couples are aware that if they keep their movements regular and in the same rhythm as their partner a mutually satisfying, simultaneous orgasm can be achieved.*

◀ *Bringing a man to the point of climax several times by masturbating him gently, and then stopping just before climax is achieved, can result in a memorable climax. It is also a therapy that helps men overcome premature ejaculation.*

The mistakes that women most commonly make are that they do not hold firmly enough, they use too slow a rhythm, or use an awkward grip. If your partner enjoys having his testes played with, there are several pleasant techniques you can use.

Scratching the scrotum is a good start – run your nails up and down. Start near the anus and then scratch up along the 'root' of the penis to the scrotum.

Next, cup his scrotum in your hand, perhaps while you do something with your other hand or with your mouth.

### SQUEEZE HIM
Now try squeezing the testes themselves. Take one between your thumb and several fingers – you

> *My fiancée is a really nice girl and I am looking forward to getting married but she thinks only of herself and her needs in bed – she never bothers much with trying to please me. What should I do?*
>
> *From what you say she is probably inhibited sexually and too shy to show her inner personality for fear that you'll find her wanting. Some women find it difficult to show any active interest in their males because they think that to do so might give the impression that they are sexually highly experienced, maybe even tarty.*
>
> *As you encourage her to do what you like best, slowly get her to talk about her sexuality with you; you will find that she will relax more. She may well have been brought up to think that a man should make all the running when it comes to sex, and could even think that you are rather strange for not wanting to do so.*

▲ *A considerate woman will watch her partner masturbate, noting how he holds his penis. This will help to ensure that when she later masturbates him, she will do so in the way that he obviously prefers.*

will find that it is very slippery and that it takes some skill to anchor it between your fingers to squeeze it. Most men enjoy increasing pressure until they ejaculate, but it can be very effective and highly exciting to 'pop' the testes between fingers and thumb. As the man becomes excited his testes will swell considerably and become tender so be careful that you do not squeeze them too enthusiastically.

### ORAL CARESSES

You can expand on the normal oral sex technique by lying astride your partner in the 69 position and using your vulva as your mouth to kiss him full on his lips. Move slowly from side to side sucking and kissing his penis as you do so. If you do not want him to climax in your mouth you can bring him off by hand or let him come between your breasts which will form an exciting channel.

### BE INVENTIVE

There are few things that turn men on more than an inventive

woman in bed. If the man is usually the one to initiate sex, it comes as a delight to have the woman take the initiative because it shows him that she has needs herself and that she is prepared to 'use' his body to satisfy them. This can have a powerful effect on most men.

Try new intercourse positions. Several studies, and clinical experience, show that men want more variety in the mechanics of intercourse. Try a new position every month or two just to keep the momentum going – surprise him with it; do not tell him in advance. Masturbate yourself in front of him – most men greatly enjoy this. Use your vibrator on yourself and use a dildo too if it turns him on. ❤

▼ *During oral sex, it is important that the woman concentrates her tongue movements on her partner's most receptive stimulatory area – the head of the penis – and that she keeps up a consistent motion with her mouth.*

# *P*LEASING A WOMAN

*The female sexual experience is very different from the male one. Understanding her likes and dislikes can do wonders for your lovemaking. But what gives a woman pleasure?*

▲ *For a woman, sex is not something that is concerned solely with her genitals – it encompasses a wide range of experiences and sensations.*

*P*robably the greatest single complaint that women have about men, sexually, is that their partners are not prepared to give enough time to them.

Women are much more variable in their approach to sex and what turns them on than men. As sexual beings they are also far superior to men. Larger areas of their bodies are sexually responsive, and many types of stimulation can be sexually arousing, and can bring them to one or more orgasms.

So, given the variable nature of a woman's sexuality, it is understandable

138

*Try as I might, nothing I do seems to turn my wife on in bed, although I have had perfectly satisfactory relationships with other women both before and after our marriage. Why do you think this should be? – she used to be very easily pleased.*

*Some women appear unable to be pleased in certain situations. Usually the problem lies within the relationship and this will need sorting out with a trained therapist or counselor. Your wife may well be resentful, or perhaps be consciously or unconsciously punishing you for something. Does she know about your dalliances outside marriage? She may be trying to clear the ground for an affair herself. Or perhaps she has fallen out of love with you for reasons which will only become apparent in therapy. You may have just become a sexual bore to her.*

*Some women in this situation are depressed or have a physical illness of some kind. Perhaps the best place to start would be with her doctor, to rule out physical or mental disease first. It's most likely a problem within your relationship though, given that she used to be sexy and now you can't please her.*

*But don't assume just because you think you have found a winning formula for pleasing a woman in your other relationships – which were probably short-lived affairs – that it is your wife's fault.*

*Take a look at your attitude towards lovemaking in general, and women in particular, and you may discover new ways to turn your wife on.*

that many men fail to explore their woman's particular sexual needs.

### TAKING TIME

A man tends to be sexually aroused quite simply and quickly – after he achieves an erection, he wants to move towards orgasm as swiftly as possible. But there are physiological reasons why this is not the case for a woman.

In her unaroused state the vagina remains tightly closed. Only after she has been caressed and cuddled and given an adequate amount of love play do the muscles of the vagina open and its walls start to pour out lubricating fluid. Only then does intercourse become easy and pleasant.

Pleasing a woman is not simply a matter of sexual technique. The man should understand and respond to what his partner wants, not because he feels that this is what is required, but because he is sensitive to her needs. He needs to be attentive, tender and loving, and he should ask what his partner wants and listen to her.

He should forget his preconceptions about what a man should or should not do. By putting her needs above his own he will not only please her but improve his own sex life as well.

### A PLEASURE SHARED

The first step towards pleasing a woman is to take a look at yourself and

▲ *The man may like to caress other parts of his partner's body, such as her feet and calves while she stimulates her clitoris.*

how you already treat her and try and improve on it. Then take every opportunity to show your love for her.

See how you could improve on your personal appearance and behavior and try behaving as you would if you had just started to go out with each other.

**▲ Many men make the mistake of concentrating solely on the most obvious erogenous zones, but most women enjoy having their whole body stimulated during the build-up to intercourse.**

### TALK AND LISTEN

A man can only really please a woman if he understands her unique sexual needs. Obviously the ideal way is to talk about what she likes and dislikes, but if she is reluctant to reveal her needs, fantasies and desires, try some gentle coaxing.

To do this it is essential to get the mood right. Kiss and cuddle a lot and get her physically aroused and relaxed. Sensual massage is a good ice-breaker but a little alcohol or looking at a sexy book or film together can often trigger off a valuable revelation.

It should not, of course, be just the woman who reveals her innermost needs in this way – both partners should try to be open with each other. It is important, too, to ensure that the person revealing his or her needs is taken seriously and not judged or condemned for their revelations. The couple should also be realistic. And if one partner does not want to reveal his or her fantasies, the other should not force the issue.

Because a woman knows what she likes best, it is obviously better that she tells you what she wants. However, even with great sensitivity, many men cannot get their women to reveal much about their sexual likes and dislikes. This could be that the woman, and the man, still

**▼ Communication is the key to good sex – partners who talk frankly about what pleases them can help each other learn what their sexual likes and dislikes are.**

hangs on to the belief that a man instinctively knows what a woman wants.

Not only does this put real pressure on a man, but some women still believe this to some extent and become annoyed when their partner does not know, as if by telepathy, what they want.

If your partner is unable, or simply does not want, to reveal what pleases her best, the next step is to learn yourself what pleases women and then to apply the lessons to your own relationship.

### GUIDELINES FOR PLEASURE

While the information contained in these steps has been gleaned through clinical experience, what pleases one woman may not necessarily please another. So be guided by your partner.

• Spend a lot of time on foreplay. Most women greatly enjoy kissing and cuddling and most need to feel loved before they can begin to enjoy themselves sexually.

• Undress her slowly, praising her body as you do so. Shower or bath together if this turns you on. In any event make sure you wash your

▲ *A pillow placed under the woman's hips raises the vagina to an angle that makes penetration by her partner easier. If he supports himself on his hands and knees, he has more control over the rhythm, and can also stimulate her clitoris.*

own genitals. Few women enjoy any form of contact with a man whose personal hygiene is poor.

• Dim the lights, but do not turn them off because being able to see each other's bodies is a turn-on itself.

• Above all, talk. Say how much you love her and how sexy her body is. Be tender and affectionate.

### OPENING FOREPLAY

Take your time and do not touch her sex organs until she is ready. Because women generally take longer to become aroused than men, this opening foreplay should be gentle and slow.

Because all women are so different in what best excites them you must always be aware of your partner's special needs.

• Watch and listen closely. The smallest grunt or moan of approval, the shift of her body, a smile and a readiness to open her legs wider are all signals to the sensitive man.

• Kiss and caress her body furthest away from her breasts and sex organs and work your way towards them over several minutes. Seek out the areas she most enjoys and concentrate on them. The feet, ear lobes, behind the

*My wife has some really weird ideas. It's all very well saying that I should do what she wants me to do, but frankly it's not easy when they go right against what I was brought up to believe in. Can you help?*

*The first thing is that your wife's 'weird' ideas might not be as odd as you think. Most of us have a very narrow experience of sex, and it's easy to imagine that just because something is unfamiliar to us it is somehow perverted.*

*It could be that you are very inhibited sexually, and that your wife's perfectly normal needs wouldn't raise an eyebrow in another marriage.*

turbate. If she is too shy to be able to do this, then here are a few tips about variations that many women greatly enjoy but might be too shy to ask for.

• Use a vibrator on her vulva or clitoris if she likes it.
• Use the vibrator in her vagina while you caress her clitoris.
• Use the vibrator on her anus while you put your fingers in her vagina and caress her clitoris with your tongue.
• Stimulate her anus with your fingertip.
• Use several fingers inside her vagina and do what she most enjoys. Some

knees, the shoulders and the insides of the thighs are very exciting for many women but are often overlooked by men.
• Caress the more erotic areas such as her mouth and bottom, still keeping away from her genitals.
• Now kiss her breasts gently. Some women complain that their man goes for them too soon and too roughly. Find what she likes and do it.
• By now she should be quite aroused and you can turn your attention to her clitoris. Use fluid from the vagina to moisten the whole area, or you can use your own saliva. Again, be guided by what she likes best. Pay attention to the length of stroke you apply, the speed and type of movement she likes, the area to which it is applied and the amount of pressure you use.
• Most women enjoy having a finger or two in their vagina when they masturbate. If she likes this, get into a position in which you can put fingers in her vagina and still carry on with clitoral stimulation.
• Bring her to a climax if she wants you to. Keep both hands and your mouth busy all the time, pleasing her.

### VARIATIONS
You can learn a lot about your partner's likes and dislikes by watching her mas-

*THERE'S NOTHING MORE OFF-PUTTING THAN MAKING LOVE WITH A MAN WHO'S IN A HURRY. SEX IS ONE OF LIFE'S MOST PLEASURABLE EXPERIENCES, SO WHY NOT TAKE TIME OVER IT?*

▲ *Some women like their whole breasts licked; others prefer their lovers to concentrate on their nipples.*

▼ *Large areas of a woman's body are sexually responsive and she can experience one or more orgasms through sensitive and attentive loveplay and intercourse.*

women just like two fingers kept still just inside their vagina while others enjoy three or four fingers being used to stretch their vaginal opening quite widely – especially when they climax.

• Your partner may enjoy her cervix being played with – you will feel this as a knob rather like the end of your nose, deep in the vagina. She may be aroused if you stimulate the front wall of her vagina with either a vibrator or your fingers. This is the G-spot area and can bring some women to a climax even without clitoral stimulation.

• Indulge in sex games that turn her on, such as dressing up or taking different roles.

The overall aim of a man who wants to bring his partner to a climax during intercourse should be to slow his response down to her rhythm. The position that a couple uses is much less important than what they actually do.

### INTERCOURSE

• Do not rush. The chances are you will come too soon if you do. Contrary to what many men and women think, violent thrusting movements are not sufficient in themselves to bring most women to orgasm.

• Stimulate the clitoris. Some positions with the man on top allow him to rub his pubic area against the woman's and bring her to orgasm this way. Alternatively you can continue rubbing her clitoris with your fingers. Some women prefer to do this themselves.

• Be appreciative. Be responsive to what she says and does. Remember her pleasure is your pleasure.

• Cuddle up to her afterwards. A common complaint from women is that after intercourse the man turns away or even goes to sleep. Hold her close and savor the feelings you both have. ♥

# PLEASURING

*Learning to give and receive sexual pleasure is an essential part of a loving sexual relationship. Luckily, this is one lesson that is easy to remember.*

Pleasuring each other, also known as sensate focus, encourages partners to concentrate on the feelings – both physical and emotional – that are produced when each gently caresses the other's body. It is widely used by many sex therapists as a method of combating a person's inability to respond sexually.

If you have sexual problems due to lack of desire, this is an excellent series of exercises. They are particularly beneficial when conducted under the guidance of an experienced therapist. Couples who are experiencing sexual difficulties, however, are not the only ones who can benefit; everyone can. These exercises are good fun and most couples will enjoy them, whether or not they have a problem. The chances are, in fact, that learning to pleasure each other will put some new oomph into even the most wonderful sex lives. It can have a surprising effect, turning mediocre sex into good sex, making great sex even better.

### WHAT TO DO

Giving someone pleasure by caressing his or her body need not be overtly sexual. It is important, in any case, that you do not have intercourse for the duration of the period for which you are doing these exercises. This may be for several weeks, but the wait should do you both good. There is nothing like practicing your ability to give and to receive pleasure for spicing things up between you.

Anticipation is, in itself, a powerful aphrodisiac.

### STAGE ONE

Practice this three times a week for at least two weeks. During this stage, you should not have any genital contact. That way there will be absolutely no pressure. You are not being asked to perform, only to experience. You cannot fail because you are not

*All photographs Rosie Gunn*

▼ *Pleasuring involves taking everything slowly and re-learning about each others' bodies and the ways to create most satisfaction.*

144

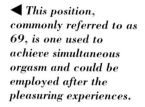

*◄ This position, commonly referred to as 69, is one used to achieve simultaneous orgasm and could be employed after the pleasuring experiences.*

being asked to succeed. Both partners should be naked. You should both feel as relaxed as possible – taking a bath together beforehand may help. Do not hurry, leave plenty of time free and make sure that you cannot be interrupted. Take the phone off the hook, and remember to put the cat out or it may decide to join in! Make sure, also, that you are both warm and comfortable.

Take it in turns to be the active or the passive partner. Alternate your roles so that the person who was the first to give pleasure during this session becomes the first to receive it at the next. The active partner should lubricate his or her hands with body lotion or oil. If either of you feels tense or unhappy with the situation, you should ask your partner to stop for a while and only resume when you feel relaxed again. If either of you feels particularly aroused and wants more it may be frustrating, but you should nevertheless avoid having sex at this stage. In cases of extreme frustration, you can always bring yourself to orgasm by masturbating.

1. To begin with, your partner should lie face downward. You can either kneel beside or sit astride him – whichever is more comfortable. Gently stroke and massage his entire body, working slowly from head to toe. You can do anything, using your hands, that you feel like doing to him. If you do anything that he doesn't like, he can show you this by gently pushing your hand away. Continue the massage for at least ten minutes.

2. Change places. It's now your turn to relax and enjoy the feelings evoked by your partner's caresses. Allow yourself to let go as much as possible and to feel each touch from your partner as fully as you can. Continue for at least ten minutes.

*▼ You may find kissing irresistible when the no-sex ban is being enforced. Any form of intimate contact is greatly enhanced.*

▲ *Massaging and touching each other all over allows you both to tune into the other's desires.*

▼ *Pleasuring involves taking time to touch every part of your partner's body. Find the places that create the most exquisite sensations.*

3. Change places and position, so that your partner is lying on his back while you massage his body and face. Do not touch his genitals. Do this for at least ten minutes.

4. Change places again so that you are lying on your back while your partner strokes your face and body. He should not touch your breasts or your genitals. Continue for at least ten minutes.

### STAGE TWO

Having practiced stage one for a minimum of two weeks, you can now progress onto stage two. Practice this stage three times a week for at least two weeks.

The emphasis at this stage is on receiving, rather than giving, pleasure. The passive partner should give his or her partner positive feedback

on what he or she finds particularly pleasurable. There is still a ban on intercourse and on genital touching.

1. Your partner should lie, face down, while you pleasure him, in the same way as before, in Stage One. But this time he should let you know what he particularly enjoys and what feels best for him. He can do this either by telling you or by guiding your hand. He should let you know not only where he likes to be touched but also how firm or gentle he prefers that touch to be. You may also kiss him wherever you wish (apart from his genitals) and he should let you

146

> **Should I orgasm or not when my lover and I are using the pleasuring technique?**
>
> *Orgasm is not the aim of pleasuring. If both partners agree that this is what they want though, and if the active partner brings his or her partner to orgasm at the end of the session, this is perfectly all right. Remember, however, that orgasm is not the point of pleasuring.*

know what he finds most pleasurable. Continue for at least ten minutes.

2. Change places and lie on your front while your partner pleasures you. You should let your partner know what feels especially good for you. Concentrate hard on what you are feeling and make sure that you transmit those

▶ *Genital pleasuring allows both partners to give and receive, and allows time to talk about preferences and desires.*

▼ *Tell your partner what you love about their body, and just how much you love and desire them.*

feelings to your partner. Once again, continue for at least ten minutes.

3. Change places and position so that your partner is now lying on his back while you pleasure his body and face. He should be letting you know what he most enjoys, telling you exactly how each touch feels, in detail. Do not touch his genitals. Continue for at least ten minutes.

4. Change places again so that you are lying on your back while your partner pleasures you. Let him know where you want to be touched and what kind of touch you most enjoy. Continue this for at least ten minutes.

5. Now, having reached the end of this session, talk to each other about what you both liked the most.

### STAGE THREE

If you feel happy with Stages One and Two after practicing for two weeks, you are ready to move on to Stage Three. This involves taking it in turns to arouse each other by touching the genitals. Once again, you should not have intercourse. You should not bring each other to orgasm. If your partner becomes too aroused and orgasm seems imminent, change your caresses to another part of their body. In this way, you can bring your partner to the brink of orgasm several times in one session. If, at any point, either of you feels nervous or tense, you should tell each other so that you can pause for a moment and turn your attention to another part of the body. Only return to this same area when you are both feeling relaxed again.

1. Lie on your back so your partner can stroke your entire body, including your breasts and nipples. He should stroke your abdomen and the insides of your thighs.

2. He should now turn his attention to your genital area. He can start by running his fingers through your pubic hair, and then concentrate on your vaginal entrance, stroking it lightly at first and then harder. He should also stroke your perineum (between vagina and anus).

3. At this point, he should begin to concentrate on your clitoris, probably a woman's most sensitive area, the very center of her sexuality. Using a suitable lubricant will help with gentle stimulation of the clitoris.

4. Change places, so that now your partner is lying on his back. Gently, using the lightest touch you can, stroke his chest, nipples, abdomen and the insides of his thighs. Run your fingers through his pubic hair.

▲ *Oral sex has a whole new meaning when it isn't meant to result in orgasm.*

5. Now turn your attention to his testicles, stroking them lightly and squeezing them gently.

6. Now it's time to begin touching his penis – center of a man's sexuality. Run your fingers up and down its length, exploring it gently to find out which are the most sensitive areas. In virtually all men these areas are the head and the frenulum – the ridge that runs along the underside.

▼ *For lubrication why not try mixing aromatic oils, carefully tailored to your sensual mood, into your massage oil.*

Stimulate his penis until he has gained a really firm erection. Then remove your hands and let his erection subside. It is bound to return when you stimulate him again.

7. Change places and guide your partner's fingers as he stimulates your clitoris. Let him know exactly what kind of stimulation you enjoy most.

8. Change places again and allow your partner to guide your hand as you stimulate his penis. He should show you exactly how he likes to be stimulated in terms of both pressure and rhythm. The clearer he can make his wishes known to you, the easier it is for you both.

Pleasuring is a sexual technique which enables partners to return to the long-lost sexual plateau of heavy petting and sexual courting. It's easy to become lazy when you have a long-term sexual partner. It's also easy to forget to continue communicating with each other, and this lack of com-

munication has the unpleasant habit of emerging only when there is a problem. Pleasuring gives you the chance to reinvent your sex life. ❤

### CASE HISTORY

**JANE:** 'HAVING HIM FONDLE EVERY SINGLE BIT OF MY BODY WAS JUST WONDERFUL. I DIDN'T HAVE TO DO ANYTHING. I JUST LAY BACK, SHUT MY EYES, AND ENJOYED EVERY MINUTE OF IT.

'ALSO, I HAD NEVER CONCENTRATED ON ANOTHER PERSON'S BODY – EVERY INCH OF IT – IN QUITE THIS WAY BEFORE. IT'S GREAT. JUST KNOWING WHAT FANTASTIC PLEASURE YOU'RE GIVING SOMEONE ELSE, ESPECIALLY IF HE TELLS YOU HOW MUCH HE'S ENJOYING IT, FEELS WONDERFUL. IT'S SUCH A LOVING, SELFLESS THING TO DO. PEOPLE SHOULD DEFINITELY DO IT MORE OFTEN.'

**ALAN:** 'WE NEVER REALLY HAD A PROBLEM ABOUT SEX. IT WAS ALWAYS GOOD, BUT NOW, SINCE WE'VE BEEN DOING THESE PLEASURING EXERCISES THINGS ARE GREAT. THEY REALLY PUT YOU IN TOUCH WITH HOW YOU FEEL ABOUT EACH OTHERS' BODIES AND – PERHAPS MOST IMPORTANTLY – HOW YOU FEEL ABOUT YOUR OWN BODY TOO. IT'S A VERY INTIMATE THING TO DO.'

▼ *Pleasuring is not something to do once and then forget about – incorporate it into your regular sexual repertoire.*

# FTERPLAY

*For some couples, falling asleep in each other's arms after lovemaking
is ideal, but for others a little gentle afterplay is the perfect ending.*

▼ *Kissing tenderly after
making love can act as
a re-enforcement
of the love bond
between the
couple.*

The popular image of afterplay as
a couple discussing art or the
meaning of life is one that few of us live
up to – or would even want to. For
most of us it merely takes the form
of a relaxing activity together –
talking or cuddling each other or
re-stimulation in preparation for
a further bout of lovemaking.

AFTERPLAY V FOREPLAY
Given that inter-
course is an inti-
mate experi-
ence, involv-

ing sharing and caring behavior, it is hardly surprising that many couples feel exceptionally close after sex. But, equally, it is fairy-tale fantasy to expect the average couple who have made love hundreds or perhaps thousands of times to be 'lovey-dovey' every time after sex.

Because it makes us aroused and is a promise of what is to come, foreplay is bound to be more important and valued by the average couple than afterplay. As with so many things in life, the preparation and anticipation is often as good or even the best part. There will never be the same excitement and drive to indulge in afterplay as there is to enjoy foreplay, and this is especially likely to be true for men who, on average, build up and resolve their sexual excitement more quickly than women.

### ANXIETY AND AFTERPLAY

There are, however, a large number of women who, either consistently or inconsistently, don't reach orgasm during lovemaking. Some find themselves

> *FED UP WITH MY OTHERWISE LOVING BOYFRIEND'S 'WHAM-BAM THANK-YOU MA'AM' APPROACH TO SEX, I FINALLY TOLD HIM EXACTLY WHAT I WANTED – THE REACTION I GOT WAS AMAZING. IT WAS ALMOST AS IF HE WAS JUST WAITING FOR THE WORD, AND HE WOULD RELEASE HIS TRUE SENSITIVE AND INCREDIBLY SEXY SELF.*

left high and dry when their partner has finished, because they feel it is somehow aggressive or wrong to tell their partner exactly what they like, where they like it and for how long.

Although some women have found various means to deal with their resulting frustration, if they were to tell their partner at the very moment of frustration, he would probably be only too eager to bring them to orgasm orally or manually – he might well be turned-on by the

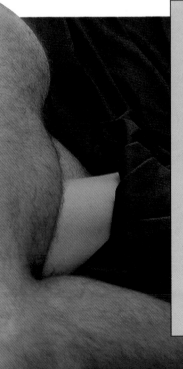

I always feel very lively and uninhibited after I make love. I want to chat about all sorts of things because I feel so much more articulate and all the things that I normally hold back just come flowing out effortlessly. My last boyfriend and I used to talk for hours after lovemaking, but my new boyfriend just wants to sleep. He says that having an orgasm makes him feel so relaxed that sleep seems a natural thing at that time. Now I'm beginning to lie awake after making love, feeling lonely and resentful and I know that eventually this will spill over into the relationship. How can I get across to him that what may seem a silly, unimportant thing to him is really a very important thing to me?

This is a problem experienced by many women, so take heart, you're not on your own. It's a difficult situation, however, because, just as you would find it difficult to change to accommodate him on this issue, then it's just as difficult for him to please you. The best you could hope to achieve is a compromise. Obviously you always make love late at night – a time when he may naturally be tired – then rolling over and going to sleep will seem the natural thing to do as far as he's concerned. Why not try making love at a different time – and somewhere other than in bed? This change in routine could solve the problem.

Many men also experience anxieties, which they may try to hide by getting sex over with as fast as possible. Some men will turn away after making love instead of using these post-lovemaking moments. It is a sad comment about the so-called 'joy' of sex that many men and women often feel they have to resort to such patterns of behavior.

### RELAX AND ENJOY IT

Given that a lovemaking session is pleasant, or even very good, most people enjoy relaxing together afterwards. A drink, listening to music, talking and cuddling are common afterplay pastimes as the couple relax in the after-glow of the sexual encounter.

None of this needs to be prolonged and formalized. The direction and nature of what happens is bound to be linked to the time of day, the mood, and the situation in which they are making love.

▲ *The best form of afterplay may be to lie in each other's arms. Then, if and when the mood takes you, you can slowly re-stimulate each other.*

prospect. Far from making the man feel vulnerable by admitting that his penis alone does not make her climax, a woman can add another dimension to sex by inviting her partner into her most intimate sexual life.

---

### RE-STIMULATING YOUR MAN

MANY MEN, ESPECIALLY YOUNGER ONES, WANT TO HAVE INTERCOURSE MORE THAN ONCE AT ONE SESSION. HERE, THEN, ARE SOME WAYS TO RE-STIMULATE YOUR MAN.

ORAL SEX IS THE BEST AND SUREST WAY OF ENSURING THAT A MAN COMES UP TO SCRATCH SECOND TIME AROUND. IF YOU ARE STILL AROUSED, YET UNSATISFIED, YOU WILL PROBABLY BE EVEN MORE WILLING THAN USUAL TO FELLATE HIM TO ENCOURAGE HIM TO PERFORM. GO GENTLY THOUGH, ESPECIALLY IF HE HAS JUST COME – LET HIM SUBSIDE FOR A FEW MINUTES. SOME MEN NEED TEN MINUTES OR MORE BEFORE THEY WELCOME ANY POWERFUL STIMULATION. CUDDLE HIM AND USE YOUR BODY TO TURN HIM ON, AND ONCE HE SHOWS SIGNS OF BEING ON THE MOVE AGAIN SPEND SOME TIME CARESSING HIS PENIS WITH YOUR MOUTH AND LIPS. FEW MEN CAN RESIST THE SOFT, MOIST APPROACH FOR LONG, AND HE WILL SOON BE READY TO MAKE LOVE AGAIN.

MOST MEN NEED MORE POWERFUL STIMULATION SECOND TIME AROUND, SO IT IS A MATTER OF EXPERIMENTING WITH THINGS YOU KNOW HE LIKES OR MIGHT LIKE. DOING THINGS TO YOURSELF CAN WORK WONDERS AND STIMULATING HIM WITH ORAL CARESSING, ANAL PLAY, 'DIRTY' TALK, AN EROTIC MAGAZINE OR BOOK, OR A SEXY VIDEO OR WHATEVER MAY DO THE TRICK.

SOME COUPLES USE THEIR FAVORITE SEX GAME AS A TURN-ON FOR SECOND-TIME SEX AND ALMOST ANYTHING THAT A SHY OR INHIBITED COUPLE FINDS DIFFICULT OR ANXIETY-PRODUCING IN NORMAL LOVE-PLAY CAN OFTEN BE INDULGED IN HAPPILY AFTER A BOUT OF LOVEMAKING HAS RELAXED THEM.

Clearly, early morning sex hardly lends itself to prolonged lying around afterwards because most people have to get up to run the house or go to work. On holiday, early morning sex can be prolonged and enjoyed in a totally different way, perhaps even used as a prelude to going back to sleep.

Relaxing afterplay can act as a reinforcement of a couple's love bond. This is a good time to compliment each other with ego-boosting remarks which are all too often left unsaid.

### SEXUAL SATISFACTION

Every lovemaking experience should leave the couple satisfied, but not satiated. Ideally, we should all be so delighted with what we have experienced that we are looking forward to the next time with eager anticipation.

Sweet nothings and praising remarks are, in this context, a part of afterplay for this time – yet foreplay for the next time. It does not really matter if it is an hour later – or a week. It serves the same purpose.

We all take our partners for

▲▼ *After orgasm, concentrate on areas other than the genitals. Nibbling your partner's ear in a mildly erotic way or tenderly drawing your finger over your partner's chest will gently relax, or excite, him.*

granted much of the time, but a few words of praise or genuine thanks for a lovely experience works wonders for a relationship, especially if one or other feels low or sexually insecure. For the woman who feels she is losing her looks or who is menopausal, or for the man who is plagued with worries about sexual inadequacy, such praise during afterplay encourages further sexual activity and boosts his morale.

It is important to stress relaxing afterplay because the vast majority or people find sex a release of ten-

## RE-STIMULATING YOUR WOMAN

UNFORTUNATELY, MANY A WOMAN WHO HAS ONE ORGASM DURING SEX AND WHO IS STILL EDGY AFTER HER PARTNER HAS COME, FAILS TO MAKE HER NEEDS KNOWN AND AS A RESULT ENDS UP FEELING CHEATED, UNFULFILLED, OR IGNORED. BUT THE MAN CANNOT BE A MIND-READER, AND SUCH A WOMAN WILL HAVE TO SPELL THINGS OUT OR GUIDE HIM INTO RE-STIMULATING HER OTHER THAN WITH HIS PENIS. FAR FROM FEELING INADEQUATE, HE WILL PROBABLY FIND IT A GREAT TURN-ON TO BE ALLOWED TO KNOW HOW AND WHEN TO 'PUSH' HIS PARTNER'S SECRET SEXUAL BUTTONS. THERE ARE MANY ALTERNATIVES, ALL OF WHICH CAN WORK WELL.

ORAL STIMULATION IS HIGHLY EFFECTIVE PROVIDED THE MAN HAS NO SCRUPLES ABOUT LICKING AND KISSING A VULVA AFTER SEX.

STIMULATION WITH THE FINGERS – EITHER THE WOMAN'S OWN OR HER MAN'S – IS A MORE COMMON FORM OF RE-STIMULATION. WHAT CAN BE VERY NICE IS IF THE MAN IN HIS POST-COITAL RELAXATION STAGE CUDDLES INTO HIS WOMAN'S BREASTS, KISSING OR SUCKING THEM AND CUDDLING HER AS SHE MASTURBATES.

A VIBRATOR OR DILDO CAN RE-STIMULATE SOME WOMEN, AND CAN BE ESPECIALLY USEFUL FOR THOSE WHO WANT A VAGINAL ORGASM BUT HAVE NOT REACHED IT DURING INTERCOURSE. FOR MANY WOMEN, HOWEVER, SUCH 'ARTIFICIAL' AIDS CAN SEEM COLD AND PRACTICAL AT THE BEST OF TIMES, BUT PARTICULARLY IN THE WARM GLOW AFTER SEX.

sions and a promoter of relaxation. As a result, many dislike further physical stimulation – unless they are unsatisfied during intercourse itself – and some find it a positive turn-off. It is probably best to leave one another's genitals and other erogenous zones alone after sex – unless, or course, you intend to re-arouse one another.

### ONCE MORE WITH FEELING

For some couples, however, a sensual episode need not end after once act of intercourse. They want to re-stimulate one another or, more often, bring the woman to orgasm to satisfy her.

Many a man finds that in stimulating his partner he becomes re-aroused himself, and before he knows it he is making love again. In fact for some women, the first bout of lovemaking will often be viewed as a form of foreplay. They

▼ *To turn your partner's mind to another bout of lovemaking, leisurely kisses on her back will both relax then arouse her after a time.*

bringing her to orgasm while he is building up to his next erection – which can often be much harder and longer-lasting than before. This way of running things can work very well even for the man who does not come too quickly, especially at the start of the day when he is fresh and full of energy and vigor.

The golden rule for this type of re-stimulation is to do exactly what the woman most enjoys. This should be all the easier if the man has already come. He will have relieved his urgent need and can then concentrate entirely on the woman and her needs – and be totally unselfish in his lovemaking.

The selfishness of men is a common complaint that women make, especially of the man who simply goes for his own pleasure and ignores her needs. Unfortunately, it is true that many men do still use their partners as a sort of sexual apparatus to satisfy their needs, although this kind of behavior is fast disappearing. ❤

let their man make love to them quickly, possibly even roughly, and then start real foreplay with a view to having an orgasm both before and during sex.

This can be a particularly good way of coping with the man who comes too quickly. The couple make love so that the man is not so 'trigger-happy'. He then spends time stimulating her and

▲ *Caressing his bottom and the area at the base of his spine will prove to be a gentle turn-on. Don't push the pace – his mind will turn to lovemaking in time.*

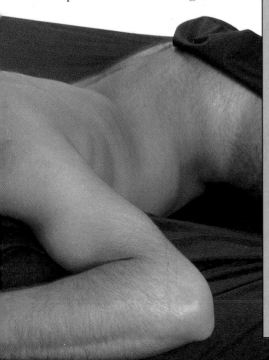

*I'm perfectly happy having one orgasm during sex – though I never come when my husband puts his penis inside me. And, because his first wife had multiple orgasms, he wants to keep on stimulating me after we have had sex. This is getting on my nerves. What can I do about it?*

*Your husband has to come to terms with the fact that he's married to you now and not his first wife. She's bound to live on in his mind, at least to some extent, and understandably, this will infuriate you. In today's sexual climate in which 'more orgasms' has come to be equated with 'sexier' women, it's easy to see why your husband behaves the way he does. He may well genuinely think that you could easily have more orgasms if you would let him help. Change will only come about if you can get it across to him that one orgasm for you is just as good and satisfying as three or four to his last wife. You will never get this across, however, if you are constantly arguing about it. It takes time and patience to convince a partner that sex is like food and that eating too much makes you ill. Be patient, the problem cannot be solved overnight.*

# 6

# Overcoming Problems

**H**owever good your sexual relationships, there may be times when things go less swimmingly. One member of a partnership may be working too hard to have time for love, or a woman might become pregnant, and find her needs have changed. There are various causes for sexual difficulties, but there are few that cannot be resolved with care and a little ingenuity. In the following pages you will find the answers to some common sexual problems, and you can take comfort from the knowledge that you are not alone in experiencing them.

# SEX IN PREGNANCY

*Everything changes during pregnancy – there are new feelings, new emotions, and new pleasures. And sex too will be different.*

Pregnancy can be a wonderful time for a couple. Many people, even today, think this is a 'no go' time sexually, but this is not so. With the worries of contraception or trying for a baby, removed, pregnancy can provide an opportunity for enjoying sex even more than before.

It is helpful when discussing pregnancy to divide the nine months into three equal trimesters. These three three-month periods differ physiologically and are usually characterized by distinct patterns of sexual behavior.

Research has found that there is a general fall in interest in the first three months, an increase in the second three months, and a dropping off as the third trimester progresses. Some studies claim that sexual desire decreases progressively as pregnancy advances.

### A LOVING PARENTHOOD

Sex during pregnancy brings a couple closer together physically and emotionally, and loving and caring for each other during pregnancy provides a strong base for

▼ *A wanted pregnancy can bond a couple more closely than any other event in their marriage ever will.*

a loving relationship with their child. It also bonds a couple together. The majority of men's first-time affairs occur during their partner's pregnancy and around the time of the birth – perhaps because they feel 'left out'. Sex in pregnancy can reassure both partners that they are still loved.

During pregnancy, both partners should be sensitive to each other's sexual needs. This might mean just cuddling, caressing, sensually massaging, or masturbating one another if either does not feel like intercourse.

But by exploring each other's body and understanding the changing needs you both

may have through the months, you will probably grow closer.

In these early months, and especially if it is a first baby, both partners will be getting used to the idea of the pregnancy and all this implies about their future life together. This will probably bring about certain changes in their sex life as well as in other areas of their relationship.

The greatest sexual advantage of pregnancy to many couples is that they do not have to use any form of contracep-

▲ *Deeply penetrative sex during the very late stages of pregnancy may, if it is accompanied by considerable stimulation of the nipples, trigger labor if the baby is overdue.*

*WE BOTH DESPERATELY WANT A BABY AND, NOW THAT I'M PREGNANT, SEX IS EVEN BETTER THAN IT WAS BEFORE. IT MUST BE BECAUSE AS PARENTS-TO-BE THERE SEEMS TO BE AN EXTRA-SPECIAL CLOSENESS BETWEEN US.*

◀ *Some pregnant women find that they feel sick or become dizzy if they have sex in conventional positions. If this is a problem, having sex in this position may help.*

husbands, and this reluctance may be accentuated during the first three months. This may cause no problem, but it really is something that is worth talking through.

Quite early in pregnancy a man can start to feel that he has served his 'usefulness' to his partner and he is no longer 'necessary' but if he is made to feel loved and wanted, he should be able to cope with a period of abstention.

### UNFOUNDED FEARS
Many people worry about sex provoking a miscarriage, but such fears are almost always unfounded. Unless the woman has a history of miscarriage, in which

tion. Some say that this unhindered, free lovemaking opens up new doors to them. But this is often offset, at least to some extent, by the hormonal, physical and emotional changes that occur during the first 12 weeks.

### CUDDLING AND HOLDING
During this stage, if any of these physical or psychological aspects are a concern, inventive couples can find other ways of showing their love and affection.

When cuddling, be gentle. Many women's breasts are very tender indeed during these early weeks of pregnancy.

### DIMINISHED DESIRE
Some women say that they make love during pregnancy only to please their

*I love my wife but I don't actually desire her now she's pregnant. Sometimes I even fantasize about other women. Am I unusual?*

*No, you're not unusual, but your wife will be feeling particularly vulnerable at this time and you must reassure her that you love her in other ways. Fantasies are fine but try not to stray from your wife.*

*Just as some women can't equate pregnancy and motherhood with sexuality, so some men make similar distinctions subconsciously. Their lover is a sexual being, but when she starts to become visibly a mother, the whole relationship is transformed. Lover becomes mother and mother is untouchable – a sexless entity just as one's own mother was. Your reactions are not uncommon and your relationship will almost certainly revert to a more physically loving one once the baby is born.*

case it is sensible to refrain from intercourse and even orgasms from weeks 10 to 14, there is nothing to worry about.

### IS THE FETUS SAFE?

At this early stage, many people think that the fetus is particularly vulnerable, and could be harmed during orgasm. Although it is true that the uterus contracts very forcibly during orgasm, there is no scientific data to prove that this harms the fetus.

It makes sense to kiss and cuddle more, to discuss your feelings about parenthood, to get in touch with each other in terms of your emotional and physical needs.

Learning how to massage your partner is a sensual experience at any time but especially useful and pleasurable during pregnancy. Two important areas are the breast and perineum.

### THE BREASTS

There is no evidence that any treatment of the breasts helps in the success of breastfeeding, but it makes sense to give a woman's breasts and nipples a lot of attention during foreplay so that she becomes used to them being sucked as a preparation for breastfeeding.

### THE PERINEUM

Perineal massage may help avoid the necessity of having an episiotomy (cutting of the perineum) on the grounds

▼ *Squatting may take practice but it allows the woman a greater degree of control.*

## USEFUL POSITIONS

DURING THE FIRST SIX MONTHS INTERCOURSE RARELY PRESENTS PROBLEMS – A COUPLE CAN MAKE LOVE IN THE WAYS THEY USUALLY DO. AFTER THIS THE SIZE OF THE WOMAN'S BUMP PRECLUDES CERTAIN POSITIONS FOR PURELY PHYSICAL REASONS. ALSO HER BREASTS CAN BECOME LARGE AND TENDER AS PREGNANCY PROGRESSES, SO LOVEMAKING POSITIONS HAVE TO TAKE THIS INTO ACCOUNT.

HERE ARE SOME PRACTICAL AND POPULAR OPTIONS FOR SEX DURING PREGNANCY.

• THE WOMAN ADOPTS AN 'ALL FOURS' POSITION. THE 'DOGGY' POSITION IS EXCEPTIONALLY GOOD AS ARE ALL REAR-ENTRY VARIATIONS.

• FOR A MORE RESTFUL APPROACH, WHEN THE WOMAN'S TUMMY IS VERY LARGE, THE 'SPOONS' POSITION WORKS WELL. IN THIS THE WOMAN LIES ON HER SIDE WITH HER LEGS DRAWN UP AS FAR AS HER BUMP WILL ALLOW. THE MAN CUDDLES INTO HER BACK AND INSERTS HIS PENIS FROM BEHIND.

• SOME PREGNANT WOMEN FIND THEY PREFER BEING ON TOP DURING SEX – PERHAPS FOR THE FIRST TIME EVER. A WOMAN'S VAGINA ENLARGES CONSIDERABLE AFTER ABOUT 12 WEEKS AND THIS PRODUCES SENSATIONS THAT ARE VERY DIFFERENT FOR BOTH THE MAN AND THE WOMAN.

• MANY WOMEN LIKE BEING UPRIGHT, ESPECIALLY LATER ON, BECAUSE THEY HAVE HEARTBURN OR FEEL DIZZY WHEN THEY LIE FLAT. THE WOMAN SITS ON HER PARTNER'S PENIS FACING AWAY FROM HIM AS HE SITS IN A CHAIR, OR ALTERNATIVELY, SHE SITS FACING HIM IF THE BUMP IS NOT TOO BIG. ANOTHER POSSIBILITY IS FOR THE WOMAN TO SQUAT ON THE PENIS AS HER PARTNER LIES ON THE BED OR FLOOR. THIS IS BENEFICIAL IN ANOTHER WAY, BECAUSE IT ENCOURAGES HER TO BECOME GOOD AT SQUATTING – A VERY USEFUL EXERCISE IN ITSELF TO OPEN UP THE PELVIS.

• VERY LATE ON IN PREGNANCY IT IS A GOOD IDEA TO USE POSITIONS THAT DO NOT INVOLVE DEEP PENETRATION. ONE POSITION THAT WORKS WELL IS FOR THE WOMAN TO LIE BACK ON THE EDGE OF A BED OR LARGE CHAIR AND PUT HER FEET FLAT ON THE FLOOR. THE MAN KNEELS ON THE FLOOR BETWEEN HER LEGS AND ENTERS HER.

that the woman is 'too small' to let the baby out. The woman lies on the floor or bed with the soles of her feet touching. Her partner then uses his fingers, well lubricated with baby oil, to massage the perineum, best done three times a week from about 12-14 weeks into the pregnancy.

From about 16 weeks onwards you can now extend the massage to include the vagina. The idea is for the man to insert two or three well-lubricated fingers into the vagina until the woman says that it is uncomfortable.

With his fingers inside her vagina he massages the perineum, encouraging the woman to relax her pelvic muscles.

It is best to insert the fingers one above the other in the early days because this stretches the vulva opening less. As time progresses the man can insert the fingers in this position but then turn them through a right angle.

The woman may experience a tingling sensation like pins and needles. When it becomes too uncomfortable, she tells him and he keeps his fingers still in that position until, after a minute or two, the intense sensations pass. He can now massage her vagina and perineum from inside.

### THE LATER MONTHS

Generally, the middle three months – the second trimester – are the best and

▲ *Rear entry positions work well during pregnancy as they put very little pressure on the woman's abdomen allowing her to enjoy sex in a relaxed and comfortable manner.*

*My breasts have started to ooze milk and I find it disgusting. I used to enjoy it when my husband kissed my nipples. I can't bear for him ever to see them now let alone touch them. Am I abnormal?*

*A little seepage is quite common, but if it bothers you then your husband should respect your feelings. I'm sure, though, that he would not be revolted by it, if that's also one of your fears. Perhaps if you keep your bra on at night you will feel less exposed and embarrassed.*

therefore the most active period sexually for both partners.

The woman, now usually through the worst of her physical symptoms, is probably beginning to feel fulfilled as a woman as the reality of the pregnancy makes itself felt, while the birth is far enough away not to be a real concern.

Some women experience more sexual drive and arousal in this second trimester than at any other time of their lives.

Most men enjoy their wives being pregnant from this stage on. Many of the changes – fuller, rounder figure, larger breasts, shiny hair, no periods, better vaginal lubrication, apparently permanently 'aroused' genitals, better skin and so on – make women more attractive. A number of these changes mimic sexual arousal.

Some men now feel at their best,

"*WHO SAID THAT COUPLES GO OFF SEX DURING PREGNANCY? TO ME, MY WIFE HAS NEVER LOOKED SEXIER AND MORE APPEALING, WHICH IS JUST AS WELL BECAUSE SHE SAYS THAT SHE FEELS PERMANENTLY SEXY!*"

especially if their self-esteem had previously been poor. The tangible evidence of their masculinity helps such men to become more at ease with their own sexuality. This enables them to relax more and to be a better partner. Similarly, many women say that from about 12 weeks onwards they feel more cuddly and physical, though not necessarily always wanting intercourse.

### COMFORTABLE SEX

The second trimester is by far the most comfortable for making love. Early problems are over and the woman's bump is not big enough to get in the way.

All the usual lovemaking positions are possible, and many women feel that because they are producing extra vaginal secretions they are ready for sex at any time.

Some women feel almost permanently sexy during these three months, with an increased need for orgasms which they claim do not leave them feeling as satisfied as they normally would.

This may be because the time taken for a woman's sex organs to return to normal after an orgasm is greatly prolonged

▼ *A little imagination can ensure an enjoyable sex life for both partners throughout pregnancy.*

during pregnancy, possibly because the whole area is so engorged with blood as a result of the pregnancy itself.

### LESS SEX

For the majority of couples, sex falls off during the last three months, and only a few carry on making love right up to the birth. The main difficulties for those who do continue making love are mainly centerd on the woman's size. The other worry that some couples have is that if they make love and the woman has an orgasm near the delivery date she will go into premature labor.

This can happen, but it is rare unless the woman has a history of premature labors. It is thought that intercourse or orgasm can trigger labor if the woman is very near delivery, and her cervix is ripe, but otherwise there is no danger. ♥

# $\mathcal{S}$EX AFTER CHILDBIRTH

*The return to sex after having a baby is a very personal matter and depends, as with all sexual matters, on both the sexual bodies and personalities of those involved.*

▲ *Kissing and caressing are loving alternatives to intercourse in the often painful weeks after childbirth. It is reassuring for both partners.*

$\mathcal{S}$ome women who have had no stitches after childbirth are back to normal sexual intercourse within a week or two, but they are the exceptions. Most women find that it is about six weeks before they feel ready to have sex again.

While waiting for intercourse to become comfortable again you can, of course, indulge in all kinds of other sexual pursuits if both of you are interested. Many women want to return to having orgasms almost immediately after birth. There is no harm in this, and it could even be positively helpful, because orgasms encourage the uterus

"*I DON'T FEEL LIKE MAKING LOVE AT THE MOMENT BUT I'M WORRIED THAT I MIGHT BE PUSHING MY PARTNER INTO THE ARMS OF ANOTHER WOMAN IF I SAY WHAT I REALLY FEEL. I JUST DON'T KNOW WHAT TO DO.*"

to return to its normal size more quickly.

Breastfeeding also makes a woman's sexual organs return to normal faster than they would otherwise. Indeed, many women who only breastfeed are able to get back to an active sex life within six weeks.

### GOING OFF SEX
For a couple who are able and inclined to go straight back to sex after a baby, all will be well. But the story is often not so simple. Having a baby is the most disorganizing event in

▲ *If intercourse is painful at this time, lovemaking can be just as stimulating through masturbation.*

▼ *After the birth it is important for a couple to literally keep in touch with each other.*

a woman's sexual life, and it affects both her and her partner profoundly – especially if it is a first child.

Very large numbers of women complain about going off sex after a baby. So many women find this happens that it has led some experts to ask whether it could even be nature's way of helping space babies out. There is no biological

▼ *Oral sex is not only satisfying for the woman but will encourage her uterus to return to its normal size more quickly.*

evidence that this is so – in countries with a traditional outlook, where women breastfeed on demand, babies are spaced out naturally, so going off sex would hardly seem necessary.

## REASONS FOR DIFFICULTIES

There are a number of reasons why so many couples have trouble with sex after the birth of a baby:

• Some women find that caring for their baby is so satisfying emotionally – and

▶ *The return to sex after childbirth is influenced by many physical and emotional factors. A couple should be aware of this and try to consider each other's needs and feelings – especially if there has been a long break.*

such a full-time job – that they simply do not have any emotional resources left to invest in their partner. As a result, he becomes ignored and sex falls by the wayside.

• Many women only feel attractive if they have a 'perfect' body image. After a baby, when they may have a bulging tummy and some stretch marks, they feel sufficiently unlovable that they cannot imagine any man wanting to make love to them.

• 'Sex is for babies and I've got a baby' is a common excuse, although unadmitted, that women tell themselves. The woman who sees sex purely as a way to have a baby – even though, consciously, she may deny that this is its only purpose – often goes off sex for some time.

• Having a baby

---

### THE EPISIOTOMY

AN EPISIOTOMY IS A CUT MADE AT THE ENTRANCE OF THE MOTHER'S VAGINA DURING BIRTH TO ENLARGE THE BIRTH CANAL TO ALLOW THE BABY OUT EASILY. EIGHT OUT OF TEN FIRST-TIME MOTHERS ARE LIKELY TO HAVE AN EPISIOTOMY – THE MAJORITY UNNECESSARILY.

EVEN A SMALL TEAR IN THE LINING OF THE VAGINA CAN BE SURPRISINGLY PAINFUL FOR SOME WEEKS AFTER CHILDBIRTH AND CAN CREATE A NEGATIVE ATTITUDE TO SEX IN THE WOMAN.

THE PAIN MAY BE ALLEVIATED IN A NUMBER OF WAYS INCLUDING: HOT AND COLD COMPRESSES, ARNICA MASSAGED INTO THE BRUISED AREA, OR HOT, SALTY BATHS THREE TIMES A DAY. BUT DO NOT BE AFRAID TO ASK FOR PAIN-RELIEVING DRUGS IF THE PAIN IS SEVERE.

REMEMBER THAT YOU HAVE A CHOICE. IF YOU DO NOT WISH TO HAVE AN EPISIOTOMY MAKE IT CLEAR FROM THE START – AND ENQUIRE ABOUT THE ALTERNATIVES SUCH AS STRETCHING EXERCISES TO REDUCE THE LIKELIHOOD OF AN EPISIOTOMY HAVING TO BE CARRIED OUT. GIVING BIRTH IN AN UPRIGHT POSITION ALSO HELPS.

of one sex, when one of the other sex was much preferred for whatever reason, can be a turn-off to some women – partly because they are highly disappointed.

• A few women are so preoccupied with the baby – its every noise, movement and smell – that they just do not have any energy left to give to their partner. Such women often overreact to the baby's behavior and worry about any problem – no matter how small.

• Fear of another pregnancy is a very common cause of going off sex at this time. About a third of all pregnancies are unplanned. It is hardly surprising,

▲ *Deep penetration can be painful for the woman. The missionary position allows the man the necessary control to make love more gently.*

therefore, if after an unplanned – and possibly unwanted – pregnancy a woman will be somewhat worried about having another.

• Post-natal depression affects a surprisingly large proportion of women, although the majority suffer only mild 'baby blues' in the first few days. True depression is a powerful force against sex at any time, in both men and women. And for the large numbers of women who do become depressed, it can badly affect their sex life.

• Tiredness is the most commonly quoted reason for going off sex after a baby, and this is certainly a real factor. Physical exhaustion from the birth, compounded by night after night of broken sleep take their toll on new mothers. One way to try to alleviate this is to have the baby in the bed with you right from the start, and to breastfeed whenever you and your baby want. This can work very well, because the baby can be fed without the mother getting up or even waking up fully – it simply lies next to its mother, snuggles in and feeds when it wants to. However, you must be certain that you and your partner are not such deep sleepers that you might inadvertently roll over and smother your baby.

This method is also unsuitable if

◄ *The weeks and months after childbirth are a good time for couples to rediscover the sensual delights of foreplay.*

"*AFTER GIVING BIRTH OUR SEX LIFE WAS FRAUGHT WITH DIFFICULTIES – BUT THEN, I'D NEVER EXPERIENCED ANYTHING SO DRAMATIC OR ANY EVENT THAT BROUGHT ABOUT SO MANY CHANGES BEFORE.*"

▼ *Oral sex, mutual masturbation, cuddling and massaging one another are all perfectly acceptable alternatives to painful intercourse.*

▼ *The woman-on-top positions allow her to control depth and penetration at this most delicate time.*

tion. While you would be very unlucky to conceive within the first month or two, it can, and does, happen.

A woman who is breastfeeding on demand will very possibly not ovulate for about 14 months if she continues breastfeeding throughout that time. However, she should be aware that even the odd bottle or, on the odd occasion, the baby sleeping through the night, can so reduce nipple stimulation that the hormones bounce back to normal, allowing ovulation to occur. ♥

either partner goes to bed having had too much alcohol to drink.

• Some women are not happy with motherhood, and resent their new lifestyle, the loss of their job and possibly their partner's attitude to them. Sex then becomes something that has landed them in a situation they now regret.

• Also, pain on premature resumption of sex can cause bad associations for the woman and put her off sex. If she has had a caesarean birth or a bad tear or painful episiotomy, anything which puts pressure on the wound will hurt. Her partner should try to be understanding about this and woo her back to the idea of sex gradually.

### DANGERS OF CONCEPTION
Whenever you return to intercourse after the birth of a child, be sure to take care with your contracep-

▼ *Although a woman may go off sex after the birth of the child, she should remember that her partner still has sexual needs.*

# WHEN THINGS GO WRONG

*When problems arise in a loving relationship, the couple's store of sexual goodwill can do much to solve any difficulties.*

▼ *Advanced lovers who enjoy inventive and satisfactory lovemaking are usually capable of sorting most problems out as they come up.*

From time to time, things can go wrong in even the most loving couple's sex life. For the man, it can result in premature ejaculation or a bout of temporary impotence, while a woman may lose her ability to have an orgasm.

Sex can be fantastic one day and lacking in magic the next. If that magic fails to re-appear during the next session of lovemaking, and then the next, the feeling of failure implants itself in the mind. That worry begins to nag away and before the couple know it they have a problem of impotence or frigidity on their hands and this can put a strain on their relationship.

The man is in a rather worse position than his partner when things start to go wrong. If a woman suddenly stops experiencing orgasm, it does not prevent her from having sex. But, if a man fails to achieve an erection or he comes too soon, the result is there for all to see. Certainly, he can make his partner come by using his hands or his mouth but for him the experience will not end in orgasm. If he does not understand his problem, the chances are that he will continue to worry even as he concentrates on his partner's needs.

### HIGH PERFORMANCE

Whether we like it or not, men are concerned about 'performance' in bed. No amount of counseling can take away from a man's mind that he is the doer, sexually. The visibility of his situation probably only makes the matter worse.

The modern male lover has a great deal to live up to. Fifty years ago and more, male performance in bed, or lack of it, was not recognized. During the

*" MY WIFE WENT OFF SEX COMPLETELY
AND WE COULD NOT FIGURE OUT WHY.
IT VERY NEARLY RUINED OUR
RELATIONSHIP. IF WE DID NOT HAVE SEX
I FELT IRRITABLE. IF WE DID, SHE FELT
WRETCHED. BUT AFTER A BREAK, I
SEDUCED HER AGAIN AS IF WE HAD JUST
MET. NOW SEX IS BETTER THAN EVER. "*

Victorian era, the sex act was over and done with much more quickly than it is today. Because the female body was always covered, men were inevitably highly aroused when it was exposed – even part of it. One popular Victorian novel describes its hero being overcome at the sight of a woman's elbow.

More importantly, sexual repression meant that men had no need for sexual technique, and a woman's satisfaction was considered irrelevant to the sex act – if indeed it was considered at all.

Nowadays, women are concerned with their own satisfaction and the man is there to ensure that this happens. In many relationships, the man puts his own satisfaction below that of his partner. The modern male stereotypes in literature and film never fail to deliver the goods – their penises are giant-sized and permanently erect, they embark on marathon lovemaking sessions where the woman's orgasms just keep on coming and their ejaculations are perfectly timed with incredible power. In reality, no man can live up to the myth.

## MODERN WOMEN'S DILEMMA

In a different way from men, the modern woman also has a great deal to live up to. Contemporary women are supposed to have a voracious appetite when it comes to sex. They are always ready and willing, their orgasms are frequent –

often they are multi-orgasmic. They love oral sex and they willingly take the lead. Add to that the well-endowed bodies portrayed in magazines – together with the endless streams of prose in agony columns and fiction promoting sexual promiscuity on one hand, with constant fidelity on the other, it is hardly surprising that the modern woman is in a sexual dilemma.

The advanced couple recognizes the myths, and has worked out where they stand, but no one is immune from this sexual propaganda. The point is we all want to be good in bed but this is not something that happens by magic. Good sex has to be learned and practiced.

A person who is experiencing short-term sexual problems can be helped by the understanding of his or her partner. If the man is experiencing difficulties, the woman can use her body, hands and

*▲ A loving partner is the best therapist. There are few problems that you cannot sort out if you tackle them together.*

mouth and, more importantly, her mind, to help him. In the same way, the man can use patience and understanding to help his partner through any difficulties that she has. A loving partner is the best sex therapist. What's more, solving sexual problems together can be fun.

### HER FOR HIM

Although there can be any number of reasons why a man may start experiencing sexual difficulties, it generally shows itself in one of two ways. Either he comes too soon, or he takes too long, sometimes not managing to come at all. The answer to either problem is not to be found in the sexual technique of his partner alone – although it is going to help. More important will be her willingness to help him overcome the problem and to turn it into a challenge they share as a couple. She will need to be prepared to talk – and then to listen. Perhaps the man needs to be reassured, flattered or spoilt. Perhaps he is worried, stressed or has a problem at work. Whatever the reason, he needs to be encouraged to communicate about it.

When the man's performance lets him down, the difficulties he is experiencing are often a result of the pressure he feels to 'perform' sexually. It is up to the woman to help reduce that pressure and,

*▼ Most of us recognize that good sex rarely happens the first time a couple sleep together. The best sex comes through familiarity.*

perhaps, make it disappear completely. The best way of doing this is to tell your partner that this is what you want to do. Tell him that he does not need to worry about your pleasure for the time being. Tell him that it is not unmasculine to lie there and let you do all the work once in a while. Love should transcend those barriers anyway.

### WHEN HE COMES TOO SOON

Most men suffer from premature ejaculation at some time in their lives. Rather than regard it as a problem, the woman can take responsibility to treat it in a number of ways. Lie your partner back and use both hands to slowly rub his penis. As his orgasm approaches, resist the temptation to rub faster and harder. Just keep the same slow rhythm going until he ejaculates. Then use your mouth to re-arouse him to make love – his next orgasm should take much longer.

Many couples are

familiar with the squeeze technique. The man should adopt a comfortable position while the woman starts to masturbate him, slowly at first, and bring him to the brink of orgasm. Then stop stimulating him and squeeze the tip of his penis firmly with your thumb over the little ridge on its underside and two other fingers on the opposite side of its rim. Squeeze hard for about 15 to 20 seconds and he should lose his erection.

### TAKING TIME

Now use your mouth on his penis as skillfully as possible and bring him back to the brink of orgasm – it should take slightly longer this time. Again, just before the point of no return, take his penis out of your mouth and squeeze it hard. If he has managed to increase the length of time before his climax approaches, use one of the woman-on-top positions and bring him to orgasm.

Continue the program. Use your mouth skillfully to revive him and, when his erection is firm, take a woman-on-top position and make love to him again. The golden rule is to ensure that he does not feel that he needs to 'perform'. If he wants you to have an orgasm

*▲ With the skillful use of the mouth and hands, a woman can overcome most of her partner's problems.*

yourself, let him use his hands or mouth – or vibrator – whichever you prefer.

The key to controlling the time of the man's orgasm during intercourse is to use a position where the woman is in control. Lie him back on the bed and straddle him and take his penis into your vagina, but only a little way. Now keep it still. Talk to him and discourage him from thinking about what you are doing which he may find too arousing.

Control any temptation to move your lower body. Now take him in a little deeper and move your buttocks slowly. At any sign of his orgasm, stop moving. If he is about to come, withdraw his penis until the sensation passes. A bonus of this technique is that many women find it very arousing.

### FAILURE TO COME

For the man who starts to experience difficulties in having an orgasm, the first thing to do is to stop conventional intercourse. Kiss and cuddle more. Your partner will be worried and you need to reassure him. When you go to bed together, practice creative foreplay but do not, in these early stages, touch his genitals. Use erotic massage and get him to do the same to you.

*I keep reading about the squeeze technique and would like to try it on my boyfriend as he sometimes comes too soon. Does it really work?*

*Yes, it does, although you will probably need to use it over several sessions, but it should give the man the encouragement that he is doing something constructive about his problem. Try not to make it all too serious, though. And vary it with stop-start intercourse as well.*

Encourage him to watch you masturbate so that he becomes aroused – allow him to bring you to orgasm like this if he wants to. Teach him what you like best. Encourage him to masturbate himself and note what gives him pleasure. Then, see if you can reproduce the sensations he has given himself. If he wants to, let him concentrate on giving you pleasure which should help to take his mind off his own sensations.

### TAKING TOO LONG

Oral sex is always an effective way of bringing a man to orgasm, especially if he is taking too long during conventional intercourse. Encourage him not to worry and just enjoy the sensations of your tongue and lips as you use them on his penis to bring him to his climax. To arouse him still further, use a 69 position where you get on top of him. The sight of your vulva should excite him. Use your hands elsewhere on his body and stroke his perineum or his buttocks.

Provided your partner is managing to maintain an erection, get him to make love to you. Explain that it is not vital for your pleasure that he comes. Use a position where he is in control and where the firmness of his erection is not too important. Lie down on the bed while he is in a kneeling position.

*Quite recently, I went off sex completely. I have a very loving boyfriend and my life seems very happy in other ways. I have not changed contraception, I am not pregnant and I am happy at work. It bothers me very much as my feelings for my boyfriend are unchanged. What can I do?*

*Although the problem may have a simple cause, your next step really should be to consult your doctor. Women – and men – do go off sex for no apparent reason and it may be that you need sexual counseling. Talk it over with your boyfriend and get him to join you. Your doctor may well suggest you both visit a specialist counselor.*

Get him to put his hands under your buttocks and lift you up to him – wrap your legs around his waist. You can move from side to side to stimulate his penis while avoiding any danger of his penis slipping out. If he fails to come inside you, use your mouth to bring him to orgasm.

### HIM FOR HER

Suddenly, after a rich and varied sex life with her partner, a woman may find that she has difficulty in

▼ *A woman's sexual potential is greater than a man's, but this means she is also more vulnerable to sexual difficulties. However, a sensitive and caring lover is the best cure and problems, once overcome, can draw you closer together.*

*MY BOYFRIEND WAS HAVING PROBLEMS
IN BED. HE CAME MUCH TOO SOON, BUT
AFTER A COUPLE OF MONTHS I TAUGHT
HIM HOW TO SLOW DOWN. NOW HE IS
THE PERFECT LOVER IN BED. HE IS
PROUD OF HIS SEXUAL PERFORMANCE.
I TAKE A QUIET SATISFACTION
IN THE FACT THAT, AS A LOVER,
HE IS MY CREATION!*

coming. There can be a host of reasons why this should be so and most can be solved with the help of a loving partner. More often than not the answer is only too simple – the form of contraception she is using, the recent birth of a baby, pre-menstrual syndrome and so on. But whatever the reason, she is going to need help and consideration from her partner to restore her sexuality.

### SEDUCE HER
To many women, lovemaking is less about sex and more about the emotional and mental approach to it. If that is right, then the rest should follow. The tried and tested means of seduction invariably work. So, take your partner out to dinner, get her to dress so that she feels good, perhaps give her a small present and concentrate on making the whole evening, as well as the loveplay, memorable. In a novel, and perhaps more romantic situation, her rediscovery of orgasm can become a real possibility.

### USE FOREPLAY
Linger on foreplay as long as you can and be inventive. Use your hands and mouth, try a vibrator or dildo or whatever you know she really likes. Kiss and caress her, talk to her and concentrate on making her feel sexy.

▼ *If you put your legs around your partner, there is little danger of his penis slipping out.*

Make taking off her clothes as sensual as you can, bathe or shower her and then, as erotically as you can, give her a massage. When you make love to her, choose a position that you know she likes, but concentrate on making the lovemaking slow and sensual. It is not one individual component but when all of them come together in the right way that will make lovemaking memorable for her. Forget your own needs – they should be satisfied by the increased level of your arousal anyway.

### CHOOSE A POSITION
Most positions have something special going for them but the side-entry position, where the woman raises her thighs and the man enters her from the side, is one of the best positions for relaxing intercourse. Use your penis and your hands to kiss and cuddle her and caress her clitoris. Tell her that you want to give her pleasure.

If the tempo needs increasing, then you can try to change the mood entirely. Let her set the pace. Lie back and get her to sit astride you, but facing away, and encourage her to use your body to give herself pleasure. Suggest that she fantasizes and uses her hands on herself to bring herself to orgasm.

Then, to set the scene for the next time you make love, use creative afterplay. After lovemaking, kiss and caress her. Tell her how much you love and want her. Kiss her breasts and, if she becomes aroused, start all over again. If you do not have another erection so soon after making love, use your mouth to bring her to orgasm. ❤

# INDEX

'69' position, 32–33, 34, 35

**A**

*à la négresse* position, 73
AIDS/HIV, oral sex, 35
anus
    intercourse, 63
    masturbation, 21, 142
    positions, 50, 70
    postillionage, 111
    prostate gland, 102–3
    vibrators, 31
arousal
    men, 132–37
    women, 139–43

**B**

banks of the Nile position, 79
bathing, 14, 113, 129–30, 131, 141
bondage, 13, 107–8, 109–10
breastfeeding, 165, 169, 171
breasts
    foreplay, 13, 14–15, 33
    oral sex, 41, 115–16
    pregnancy, 160, 161
    vibrators, 31
buttocks
    foreplay, 11, 12, 13
    vibrators, 31

**C**

CAT (coital alignment technique), 57
childbirth, 70–71, 80, 153, 164–69
clitoris
    intercourse, 49, 68
    masturbation, 20, 26, 30, 114, 142
    oral sex, 32–33, 39, 41, 42, 44–45
    water, 21
clothes
    fantasies, 12, 14
    foreplay, 29, 107
    quickie sex, 107, 119, 120–21
    stripping, 113–14, 133
coital alignment technique (CAT), 57
conception, 56, 70, 169
contraception, 134, 159–60, 169
*cuissade* positions, 73–74
cunnilingus, 34, 35, 38–45

**D**

'doggy' position, 61, 62–64
dressing up *see* clothes

**E**

ejaculation
    *see also* premature ejaculation
    delay, 74–75, 88, 113
    oral sex, 37–38
episiotomy, 71, 161–62, 166

**F**

fantasies
    dressing up, 12, 14
    foreplay, 28–29
    masturbation, 19, 25–26
    women, 89, 95, 140
feathers, 108–9
fellatio, 34–35, 36–38, 131, 152
femoral intercourse, 108
    *flanquette* positions, 72–73
Florentine sex, 74–75
foreplay, 10–45, 114–15, 141–43
    for her, 29–31, 141–43, 154
    for him, 29, 31–32, 135–38, 152
    masturbation, 16–27
    re-stimulation, 152, 154–55
frenulum, 37, 114, 116, 148
frigidity, 88
'frog' position, 75, 80
furniture, 77

**G**

G spot, 98–103
    *see also* prostate gland
    man-on-top positions, 80, 100–101
    rear entry positions, 60, 61, 89, 96
    side-by-side positions, 68
    women-on-top positions, 49, 51, 101
games, 11–12, 109–10

**H**

HIV/AIDS, oral sex, 35
hygiene, 12, 36, 141

**I**

ice, 107, 109
impotence, 170, 172, 173–74

**K**

*Karma Sutra*, 58, 72, 77
kissing
    foreplay, 11, 12, 14, 15, 31, 40–45, 115–16
    genital, 15
    man-on-top positions, 55–56
    women, 141–42

**L**

lubrication, 27

**M**

man-on-top positions, 54–59, 72–73, 78, 79, 80, 81–82, 95
massage
    breasts, 14–15
    foreplay, 30, 107, 108–9, 130
    penis, 13
    pleasuring, 145–46
    pregnancy, 161–62
masturbation, 16–27
    female, 17–19, 20–21, 22–23, 141–43
    male, 17, 19–20, 135–37
    sharing, 22–27, 135–37, 141–43
    simultaneous orgasm, 95
menstruation, 41, 122
missionary position, 54–57, 78, 95, 100

**O**

oral sex, 15–16, 32–33, 34–45, 137
    *see also* cunnilingus; fellatio
    AIDS/HIV, 35
    foreplay, 15–16
    positions, 42–45
    re-stimulation, 152, 154
orgasm, 86–103
    delay, 26, 29–30, 52–53, 75–76, 90–91
    female, 17–18, 29–31, 86–87, 107
    G spot, 99–100
    male, 31, 86, 106–7
    multiple, 21
    simultaneous, 10, 57, 86–97
ovaries, stimulation, 58, 59

**P**

'parting of the Waves' position, 82
penis
    intercourse, 97
    massage, 13
    masturbation, 19–20, 26, 135–36
    oral sex, 32, 37, 109–10, 131
    stimulation, 135–37
perineum
    foreplay, 12, 13, 14, 32, 111
    oral sex, 32–33
    pregnancy, 161–62, 166
plateau, 13, 116
pleasure
    men, 133–37
    women, 138–43
positions
    G spot, 51, 60, 61, 80, 96, 100–101
    man-on-top, 54–59, 72–73, 78, 79, 80,

81–82, 95
    oral sex, 42–45
    pregnancy, 53, 55, 62, 67–68, 69, 161
    problems, 175
    rear-entry, 60–65, 73–74, 78, 79, 81, 89,
      100–101
    romantic sex, 56–57, 130–31
    side-by-side, 65, 66–71, 78–79, 117
    side-entry, 69–70, 89–90, 95–96, 175
    simultaneous orgasm, 95–96
    standing up, 76, 77, 79
    woman on top, 48–53, 65, 74–76, 78,
      80–81, 96–97, 101, 116–17
postillionage, 111
pregnancy, 158–63
    positions, 53, 55, 62, 69, 70–71, 81, 161
premature ejaculation, 52–53, 57, 89, 170,
172–73
problems, 170–75
prostate gland, 98, 102–3

**Q**

quickie sex, 70, 79, 118–23

**R**

'reach for the Sky' position, 81–82
rear-entry positions, 60–65, 73–74
    G spot, 100–101
    simultaneous orgasm, 89
    variations, 78, 79, 81
romantic sex, 56–57, 126–49
    for her, 130–31, 138–43
    for him, 131, 132–37
'Rutting Deer' position, 57, 81–82

**S**

sensate focus, 144–49
showers, 11, 12–13, 21, 114, 115
side-by-side positions, 65, 66–71, 78–79, 117
side-entry positions, 69–70, 89–90, 95–96, 175
    *soixante neuf*, 32–33, 34, 35
spanking, 11, 13–14, 110–11
'spoons' position, 65, 67–69
squeeze technique, 52–53, 88, 173
'stagecoach to Lyon' position, 76–77
standing up positions, 76, 77, 79

**T**

testicles
    intercourse, 72
    oral sex, 37, 131, 136–37
tongue bath, 15

**V**

vagina
    G spot, 98–101
    masturbation, 20, 30, 114, 142–43
    oral sex, 38–39, 44–45
verbal foreplay, 11, 14, 114
vibrators, 109
    foreplay, 12, 15, 30–31, 94–95, 109, 142–43
    masturbation, 20–21, 23
    positions, 44, 71
    re-stimulation, 154
'Viennese Oyster', 74
vulva, oral sex, 38, 41, 44–45
    masturbation, 20, 30

**W**

'wheelbarrow' position, 76
'Wild Geese' position, 81, 83
woman-on-top positions, 48–53, 65, 74–76,
116–17
    simultaneous orgasm, 96–97
    variations, 78, 80–81

**X**

'x' position, 75–76

*Index compiled by INDEXING SPECIALISTS, Hove.*

176